Sisters in Crime

Also of Interest

Raymond Chandler by Jerry Speir

P.D. James by Norma Siebenheller

John D. MacDonald by David Geherin

Victorian Masters of Mystery: From Wilkie Collins to Conan Doyle
by Audrey Peterson

Ross Macdonald by Jerry Speir

The Murder Mystique: Crime Writers on Their Art edited by Lucy Freeman

Dorothy L. Sayers by Dawson Gaillard

Sons of Sam Spade: The Private Eye Novel in the 70s by David Geherin

Murder in the Millions: Erle Stanley Gardner—
Mickey Spillane—Ian Fleming by J. Kenneth Van Dover

Rex Stout by David R. Anderson

Dashiell Hammett by Dennis Dooley

The American Private Eye: The Image in Fiction by David Geherin

13 Mistresses of Murder by Elaine Budd

The Secret of the Stratemeyer Syndicate: Nancy Drew, the Hardy Boys,
and the Million Dollar Fiction Factory by Carol Billman

Michael Innes by George L. Scheper

The Literature of Crime and Detection:
An Illustrated History from Antiquity to the Present
by Waltraud Woeller and Bruce Cassiday

James M. Cain by Paul Skenazy

Sisters in Crime

FEMINISM
AND THE CRIME NOVEL

◆ ◆ ◆

Maureen T. Reddy

◆

A Frederick Ungar Book

CONTINUUM ◆ NEW YORK

1988

The Continuum Publishing Company
370 Lexington Avenue
New York, NY 10017

Printed in the United States of America

Library of Congress Cataloging-in-Publication Data

Reddy, Maureen T.
    Sisters in crime : feminism and the crime novel / Maureen T.
Reddy.
        p.   cm.
    "A Frederick Ungar book."
    Bibliography: p.
    Includes index.
    ISBN 0-8264-0407-3
    1. Detective and mystery stories, American—Women authors—History
and criticism. 2. Detective and mystery stories, English—Women
authors—History and criticism. 3. Crime and criminals in
literature. 4. Feminism and literature. 5. Women and literature.
I. Title.
PS374.D4R4 1988
813'.0872'093520—dc19   88-20255
                                                              CIP

Contents

Acknowledgments

Many friends and colleagues contributed to my thinking about the intersection of feminism and crime fiction. I appreciate their lively interest and think fondly of our discussions and arguments. I especially want to thank Brenda O. Daly, Sara Ruddick, Deborah Roberts, Eileen Schofield, and Penny Zezima, each of whom discussed this project with me at one stage or another and frequently recommended books and authors. The women at Womankind books in New York offered "mini-reviews" by phone of lesbian novels that might interest me; I am grateful to them for pointing me toward books I might otherwise have missed. My colleagues in the English Department at Rhode Island College heard and commented on a draft of portions of chapters three, five, and six; Joan Dagle, Judith Mitchell, and Carolyn Swift offered particularly helpful suggestions. Many thanks also to Linda Gardiner, editor of *The Women's Review of Books,* for inviting the review essay that eventually became the germ of this book and for permission to incorporate parts of that piece, which appeared in the December 1987 issue, into chapter one. Valerie Miner very generously read and offered criticisms of an earlier version of chapter six; her thoughtful comments were a great help. I am grateful also to Bruce Cassiday and Evander Lomke of The Continuum Publishing Company, who read the *Women's Review* article and approached me about doing this book, for their encouragement and for their excellent editorial suggestions.

Without the help of my parents, Thomas and Joann Reddy, who provided lots of free babysitting and unstinting support, and of my husband, Douglas Best, who tracked down out-of-print novels by scouring mystery bookstores in three cities and often took on the entire burden of childcare and household work, I could not have written the book. My sister, Ann Marie Reddy, talked with me endlessly about crime novels, found an able typist in Anne Starr and acted as courier between us, helped prepare the list of works cited, proofread the manuscript, and generally made (and makes) my life easier and happier. This book is dedicated to her, in loving sisterhood.

1

A Sisterhood of Detection

If you visited Kate's Mystery Books in Cambridge, Massachusetts, in the summer of 1987, and headed into the second room, past the shelves built by Robert B. Parker and toward the chair holding a skull, you would have found a section labeled "Strong Women Detectives." Before a rogue MBTA bus rammed into Kate's and forced a temporary closing, the "strong women" section took up a good-sized portion of a bookcase, with a wide spectrum of authors and subgenres represented among the books cramming the shelves and spilling out onto the floor. While some customers ignored the section and others made feeble jokes about it ("Where's the section on weak male detectives?"), many more stopped to browse and then to buy. Most of the books housed here were written by women and published within the past decade. Although there were many strong women authors of detective fiction long before then—Dorothy L. Sayers, Agatha Christie, Margery Allingham, and Ngaio Marsh spring instantly to mind— most of their detectives were male or, if female, hardly in the "strong woman" category. Now, however, you can choose among Sue Grafton's Kinsey Millhone and Sara Paretsky's V. I. Warshawski, both professional private investigators; Antonia Fraser's Jemima Shore and Anne Morice's Tessa Crichton, actors/television celebrities who moonlight as amateur detectives; Amanda Cross's Kate Fansler and Susan Kenney's Roz Howard, college professors prone to entanglement in murder mysteries;

1

Lucille Kallen's Maggie Rome and Barbara Wilson's Pam Nilsen, involved both in publishing and in detection; and, perhaps least foreseeable even a decade ago, Susan Dunlap's Jill Smith and Katherine Forrest's Kate Delafield, police detectives, homicide division.

The increasing diversity of female protagonists of crime novels reflects recent social changes, with perhaps the most important influence on the genre being feminism. Just as actual women have moved into previously all-male preserves, ranging from the academy to the police force, so have their fictional counterparts taken advantage of these new opportunities. Some male writers have recently focused on female detectives, but their ranks are thus far minuscule, and not altogether praiseworthy, vide Modesty Blaise. For this and for other reasons that should be clear by the end of this chapter, I limit my attention in this book to women mystery writers who have created female protagonists of series, particularly those feminist writers at the forefront of an emerging countertradition in crime fiction. The basic features shared to varying degrees by novels in this countertradition are the violation of linear progress, the ultimate absence of authority as conventionally defined, and the use of a dialogic form.[1] This countertradition shares with feminist work in other genres an essential subversiveness, with women writers borrowing familiar features of detective fiction in order to turn them upside down and inside out, exposing the genre's fundamental conservatism and challenging the reader to rethink his/her assumptions.

Rethinking assumptions is an activity valued by both crime-fiction readers and feminists, and so I want to clarify some of my own assumptions here, especially because there are so many competing definitions of both crime fiction and feminism to be had. Throughout this book, I'll be working with the broadest possible definitions of both. No matter how broadly defined, though, the terms *feminist* and *crime fiction* may seem wildly incompatible, nearly oxymoronic. Many feminists recoil from murder mysteries, convinced they will find no pleasure in tales of crime and punishment, while many crime-novel aficionados see the infusion of a particular ideology as certain to reduce their pleasure in the genre. Both of these positions rest on false assumptions, with the former assuming that all crime novels are both violent and socially conservative and the latter assuming that the best crime novels do not advance any ideology at all. Every novel, of whatever genre, is suffused with *some* ideology; it's just that one doesn't usually notice the ideology in a work of fiction if it is compatible with culturally prevalent beliefs. This is not to say that most crime novels are nonviolent and socially liberal or that no feminist crime novel is marred by didacticism, but that both crime novels and feminism come in more varieties than those who view the two as incompatible would admit.

Anyone now writing about crime fiction ventures into a sort of literary funhouse, where specters of controversy past, present, and future threaten to pop out at any moment. The central ongoing debates revolve around the issue of genre boundaries: should the crime novel be treated as a distinct genre, separate from other forms of fiction? Some critics take what might be called a "popular culture" approach, arguing that what is most important about the crime novel is its very difference from more established, respectable kinds of fiction, while others insist that crime novels ought to be treated precisely as one would any other work of fiction. Then there is the question of what to call this literature: detective fiction? mystery? crime fiction? murder mystery? thriller? A number of critics, along with many writers of detective/crime/mystery/thriller novels, maintain the importance of clear distinctions among the subgenres, with some arguing that only a fraction of the books published under the category each year may properly be called "detective fiction."

Purists still pledge their fealty to the tenets set down by the Detection Club in Britain in the 1930s, which in turn followed Ronald Knox's "Ten Commandments of Detection" in requiring members to abjure "Divine Revelation, Feminine Intuition, Mumbo-Jumbo, Jiggery-Pokery, Coincidence or the Act of God" and to have their detectives solve crimes strictly through processes of deduction, relying on clues presented fairly to the reader. The main interest in detective stories that conform to such rules focuses on the process of solving the puzzle, with character and personal relationships largely extraneous to the plot. Indeed, Dorothy Sayers, who led the Detection Club for many years, criticized writers whose detectives fell in love during the course of an investigation or who were otherwise at all distracted from the business of solving the crime, arguing that such forays into complex characterization marred the "Aristotelian perfection" of the form. Of course, Sayers broke her own rules, as did many members of the Detection Club, but that is a different story. By the standards of the Detection Club and its followers, most novels that fit the definition of detective fiction were written forty or more years ago. What most of us read now, plucked from the "mystery" or "detective" shelves of our local bookstores, might best be called crime novels, where the puzzle is not the sole interest, but may be subsidiary to character or to an investigation of social conditions.[2]

The debate about terms and categories goes on apace, despite the evident unhelpfulness (and impracticality) of sharp genre distinctions. Those who would define the detective story most rigidly overlook the varieties of pleasure readers may seek from crime fiction. Although many readers greatly enjoy the sheer intellectual exercise of amassing clues and trying to beat the detective to the puzzle's solution, that is probably not the sole reason they read crime fiction. They sometimes turn to crime fiction for precisely the same reasons they read other kinds of literature: escape, enlightenment, enjoyment of felicities of style and characterization, and so on. Why then insist that each kind of pleasure be compartmentalized, isolated from the others? None of this passion for categorization is truly new, nor is it restricted to the crime novel, although crime fiction's fairly recent admission as a suitable subject for scholarly research has certainly enlivened the old debate by injecting into it the academic love of classifying, labeling, and judging. To support these attempts at codification is to contribute to the establishment of a canon of detective fiction and to define many novels as noncanonical; unsurprisingly, that canon is overwhelmingly masculine, paralleling canonical literature of other genres. Agatha Christie, Dorothy L. Sayers, and Ngaio Marsh are the equivalents here of Jane Austen, Charlotte Brontë, and George Eliot: those women almost always admitted to the ranks of "important writers," with a sort of guest chair sometimes available for the addition of a fourth woman, usually P. D. James or Ruth Rendell (à la Virginia Woolf or Emily

Brontë).[3] Sexist bias masquerading as objective, aesthetic judgment is rampant in literary criticism, as so many feminist critics have shown,[4] and the field of crime fiction is not exempt.

One useful way to counteract the marginalization of women's writing in any genre is to redefine the center; in this case, I would argue for a broad definition of crime fiction, using the term as an inclusive one covering all those works of fiction in which a central interest lies in the examination of events, often but not always criminal, that are partly concealed at the beginning of the story. A murder or even a crime of any sort is not strictly necessary, nor must the solution to the problem be contained in physical clues, as detective purists claim. Frequently, in the most interesting mysteries and particularly in those written by women, the answer lies in character, with its revelation depending upon the investigation of personality and on the conjunction of the personal and the social. That said, it would be absurd not to acknowledge the frequency with which murder occurs as the event that requires examination in crime fiction. The taking of human life is the ultimate crime, the one transgression against moral law that no society can ignore. The act of murder serves the crime novelist as both fact and metaphor, plot device and theme, drawing readers into the novel by engaging the reader's interest in the extremes of human passion. There are very few other crimes that hold attention in quite the same way, which explains why crime novels seldom focus on burglary or election fraud—although some certainly do.

Even though women have been writing crime fiction for nearly a century, the genre seems a particularly problematic one for the woman writer because of its history. As I have explained, the form has been fairly rigidly defined according to a masculinist model, by which "objective," distanced rationality is the highest virtue; crime novels tend to celebrate traditionally masculine values and to reinforce conservative social attitudes. The classic crime novel begins in disorder or in violation of order and proceeds more or less linearly to order; it is therefore essentially reassuring, its message proclaiming that it is not only desirable, but actually possible, to banish or to destroy disruptive social elements, and that the greatly to be desired continuation of bourgeois, patriarchal society depends upon general acceptance of the control of a masculine authority figure who is alone capable of explaining the world satisfactorily. The detective novel, in particular, is basically monologic in form: although we may at first think we are hearing many voices with varying perceptions of reality, one voice silences all the others, finally establishing a single version of reality, which he calls "truth," that we are required to accept if we are to move with the text toward closure.

Like most of their male colleagues, women crime novelists have tended to use a figure representing moral authority, a controlling intelligence who explains what at first has seemed inexplicable, as the main character in their books. This person may be a professional detective (police or private) or a gifted amateur, but is more frequently male than female, witness Sayers's Peter Wimsey, James's Adam Dalgliesh, Allingham's Albert Campion, Rendell's Chief Inspector Wexford, Catherine Aird's C. D. Stoner, or Martha Grimes's Richard Jury and Melrose Plant. If the woman detective in crime fiction remains relatively rare, the female series character is rarer still. One possible reason for this is that employment discrimination on the basis of sex has barred women from jobs as police detectives or private investigators until fairly recently, leaving crime novelists who wanted plausible female protagonists with only the option of gifted amateurs, like Christie's Miss Marple. Another possibility is that writers interested in reaching the largest possible audience have tended to choose a male protagonist over a female, on the principle that women will read novels by and about men but not vice versa (girls read the Hardy Boys series but few boys would want to be caught with a copy of a Nancy Drew book in their hands—cultural bias dies hard). Then, too, the whole notion of a woman in charge, and especially a woman presumably dedicated to ideals of law and order, works against traditional expectations. The many books now available featuring strong women detectives suggest that some expectations may be shifting—there is obviously a large readership for these books or fewer would see print—but reading a sampling of these books shows that the conventions themselves are alive and well. Far too often, strong women detectives are found filling the (gum) shoes of strong male detectives, with only the gender changed.

Leaving the role of detective unaltered but for gender is the hallmark of the woman writer working within narrowly defined genre limitations, themselves the products of an incomplete literary history. The generally accepted history of crime fiction goes something like this: the first murder mystery is Edgar Allan Poe's "Murders in the Rue Morgue" and the first series detective is Arthur Conan Doyle's Sherlock Holmes, with these two prototypes influencing all subsequent crime fiction, which reached a kind of apex in Britain between the wars in the heyday of the Detection Club and in the US in the 1920s with the emergence of a distinctively American variant of the form in the pulp magazines. The various mutations of crime fiction now popular certainly owe something to these predecessors, but this version of the history of the crime novel excludes as much as it includes, just as pre-1975 (and some later) theories of the rise of the novel overlooked significant feminine contributors to the genre's development. Dale Spender, Elaine Showalter, and other feminist critics have labored to uncover the previously obscured history of the novel, bringing back to light literally hundreds of forgotten women novelists of the eighteenth and nineteenth centuries who were enormously popular in their own day and whose influence has since been grossly underestimated (if estimated at all).[5] I think crime fiction is ready for a revised history as well, one that will give as much attention to the influence of gothic and sensation novels on crime fiction as the current history accords Poe and Doyle. Although tracing the history of the crime novel lies well beyond the scope of this book, I want to sketch the outline of an alternative literary history here. For the roots of feminist crime novels, one must look back to the gothic novels of Ann Radcliffe and her sister writers who, in turn greatly influenced the female sensation writers of the 1860s, such as Mrs. Henry Wood, whose *East Lynne* (1860–61) has recently returned to print.

Mrs. Henry Wood, Wilkie Collins, and Mary Elizabeth Braddon are generally considered the originators of the sensation novel (Hughes, p. 109), a genre that descends from the enormously popular gothic novels of the eighteenth century. Both gothic and sensation novels concern themselves with secrets and mysteries, violence and fear. Significantly, both genres were dominated by women authors (Spender, pp. 230–243; Hughes, pp. 28–30) and both place women's position in society at issue, examining the terrifying underbelly of the apparently placid domestic haven idealized by official culture. Gothic novelists conduct this examination by portraying the heroine as victimized and terrorized by men, but ultimately victorious; in Ann Radcliffe's *The Mysteries of Udolpho* (1794), for instance, the heroine is persecuted by her aunt's villainous husband and held prisoner in his remote castle, but eventually gains both freedom (of sorts) and love. Sensation novelists, on the other hand, create female villains whose criminality stems from the same sources as the gothic heroine's victimization. Braddon's *Lady Audley's Secret* (1862), for example, features a heroine whose crimes all result from her inability to earn a living and her consequent need to find a husband. Lady Audley abandons her son, commits bigamy, shoves her first husband down a well in hopes of killing him, considers poisoning her second husband, and sets a fire that kills a man not because her acculturation has failed, but because it has succeeded all too well. As Elaine Showalter puts it in *A Literature of Their Own*, the shared secrets of sensation novels "were the secrets of women's dislike of their roles as daughters, wives, and mothers" (p. 158) and "Lady Audley's real secret is that she is *sane* and, moreover, representative" (p. 167). If gothic novels are about women's fears, as Tania Modleski suggests (p. 20), then sensation novels are about their fantasies, with both encoding strikingly similar critiques of women's entrapment in domestic life and powerlessness in their primary reality, the family.

In *The Madwoman in the Attic*, Sandra Gilbert and Susan Gubar argue that the concerns of gothic and sensation novels I have sketched here are actually repetitions of "the paradigmatic female story," a drama of "imprisonment and escape" in which domestic spaces serve "as primary symbols of female imprisonment," with this story "reflect[ing] the literal reality of [the women authors'] own confinement in the constraints they depict" (pp. 85–87). Gilbert and Gubar trace this story through the works of Mary Shelley, Jane Austen, Charlotte Brontë, George Eliot, and other women writers not usually linked with the gothic and sensation genres. The forms in which female gothic and sensation writers inscribed the "paradigmatic female story" are immediately recognizable as precursors of the modern crime novel—at least one male critic describes *The Mysteries of Udolpho* as "the first successful thriller"[6]—but these earlier novels have been systematically devalued and, as a consequence, many are lost (Spender, p. 243). Current women writers of crime fiction belong on a continuum that begins with the writers of female gothic and that occasionally intersects with the continuum that includes Poe and Conan Doyle. A feminist tracing of the history of crime fiction would acknowledge literary foremothers as well as forefathers.

I've been using the terms *feminist* and *feminism* without definition to this point, partly because defining feminism presents a challenge as great as defining crime fiction: the feminist movement is far from monolithic. Most dictionaries define feminism as a doctrine advocating social and political rights for women equal to those of men, but this is only a partial definition, as from this desire for equality has sprung a complex revisioning of woman's nature, history, and role and, concomitantly, a similar revisioning of man's nature, history, and role. For the purposes of this study, I am using *feminism* to mean a way of looking at the world that places women's experiences at the center. It sees women as capable of intelligence, moral reasoning, and independent action, while also giving attention to the multivarious social, legal, and psychological limitations placed on women by the patriarchal societies in which most live. Feminism is always aware of the complexity and diversity of women's lives, especially those dissimilarities arising from differences of class, race, and nationality; however, it also insists that within this pluralism is a shared core of experience that is overlooked only at peril. Feminism asserts that women may indeed be different from men, but that few of these differences are biologically determined and that *different* ought not be used as a code word for *lesser*.[7] Carol Gilligan's landmark study of women's ways of thinking, *In a Different Voice*, and Nancy Chodorow's exploration of the sociology of gender in *The Reproduction of Mothering* undergird the present study. Taken together, Chodorow and Gilligan suggest that men tend to define themselves through individuation and separation, valuing autonomy over connections with others and perceiving relationships in terms of rules and procedures for adjudicating issues of individual rights, whereas women tend to define themselves in terms of relationships, valuing affiliations with others over autonomy and perceiving relationships in terms of balancing needs and negotiating responsibilities in order to maintain the relationship.

If women, because of their socialization, read the world rather differently than do men, as feminist theorists like Gilligan and Chodorow assert, then it stands to reason that a woman detective might read clues differently than a male detective would and that her relationship to the problem presented would differ from the male detective's. The detective, whether male or female, is primarily a reader, but a reader more than ordinarily sensitive to nuances of meaning and to implications. The text presented to the detective is a fragmented one, with the detective taking on the task of both reading and writing this text: he/she takes the signs presented (clues) and, eventually, turns them into a coherent narrative, making the text of the crime whole again and the actual text whole and fully legible for the first time. When Nero Wolfe or Spenser exposes a criminal, he does so through a reconstruction of the previously obscured crime narrative, putting together who did it, how, and why. His is the privileged voice, the one that tells the other characters and the reader of the novel what the text means. However, what the closure of detective fiction generally won't admit is precisely what the earlier portions of the novel rest upon: narratives, and the signs of which they are composed, are capable of supporting multiple, conflicting interpretations. Could the detective's solution simply be another misreading, albeit the ultimate misreading? To what extent ought one trust the detective's reconstruction of the crime narrative? In conventional crime fiction, the answer is "entirely," but women writers, and especially feminist women, might be expected to play around with the issue of narrative authority and to be at least somewhat distrustful of authority generally. However, just as some women entering institutions like law or medicine adopt a male model of behavior in order to succeed, so do many women crime novelists follow conventional formats.

The field of crime fiction is of course an institution, with its own history, traditions, and even rules, its insistence on self-definition and self-regulation, its great names and its enfants terribles. It is perhaps more flexible than law or medicine, but it is an institution nonetheless. Has the influx of women writers with women detectives changed the genre, or has this influx been in the nature of a process of adding in? Have the rules changed or do they remain the same, with different players at the game? Both, I would argue. A few women writers have recently ventured into the previously exclusively masculine preserves of the police procedural, while others have created gun-toting, unsentimental, tough-talking female loners in the hard-boiled tradition of professional investigators. All of these novels implicitly question, and undermine, received wisdom about gender-specific character traits and abilities, but many are not otherwise remarkably different from masculine models of the subgenres. Lillian O'Donnell's numerous novels featuring Norah Mulcahaney of the NYPD, for instance, offer occasional criticisms of the antiwoman policies of police departments, but these are merely asides, minor divergences from a familiar path toward order and justice as traditionally defined. Norah, despite her unconventional job, is a patriarchal woman and the novels focusing on her are patriarchal texts. On the other hand, Sara Paretsky's V. I. Warshawski novels have become increasingly feminist and subversive. In the earlier novels, Paretsky's narrator-protagonist incorporates feminist critiques into her tales, but the plots and themes of the novels are fairly conventional. In *Deadlock*, for instance, Warshawski reflects on why she refuses to divulge her first name to new acquaintances, noting that offering only her initials prevents the instant familiarity that deprives women of dignity when all females are Janet, Lois, etc., but males are Mr. Jones, Mr. Smith, and so on. Nevertheless, the crime that V. I. investigates in *Deadlock*—murder to cover embezzlement—is not one that leads to many feminist questions, unless the reader steps away from the novel to ask what might make a man value a shipping company over human life or a woman prize economic security over love or integrity. Such questions hover on the periphery of Paretsky's text, where it is possible to ignore them without diminishing the impact of the murder mystery itself. Also on the periphery, but nonetheless significant, are Warshawski's intense friendship with a woman doctor and a romanticized attachment to her dead mother. In the most recent Warshawski novel, *Bitter Medicine*, Paretsky moves feminist concerns from the edges of the text to its center, fusing Warshawski's personal and professional lives as she investigates the death of a friend and attacks by a so-called right to life group on her friend Lotty's clinic, and thereby demonstrating the truth of the feminist axiom that the personal is political. Whereas the O'Donnell novels change only the gender of the police procedural's protagonist, Paretsky's *Bitter Medicine* redraws the boundaries of Hammett/Chandler/MacDonald territory while forcing readers to reconsider their usual reading strategies in order to make sense of the novel.

Readers of detective fiction and fictional detectives themselves have learned these reading strategies in a system that teaches everyone to read as men.[8] For the most part, crime fiction *must* be read in this way to be at all satisfying. It is this, I think, that causes feminists to feel guilty about the pleasure they derive from reading crime fiction. For the duration of the novel, they must suspend their feminist sensibilities, hold them in abeyance, in order to understand the text properly, to look forward to the demystification of the fragmented narrative and to its reconstitution by some designated (usually male) authority, with the apprehension of the criminal and his/her being brought to justice, as defined by the detective and/or by the masculinist legal system, a near certainty. What happens if feminists refuse this suspension of feminist sensibilities, if they insist on reading as women? Some books resist such a reading, falling apart as the reader refuses the author's guidelines for interpretation. Other books, though, become richer, more interesting, when read from a female vantage point, which is true of Dorothy L. Sayers's *Gaudy Night*, the first feminist detective novel and the book most feminist readers of crime novels I know cite as the one that first attracted them to the genre.

In *Gaudy Night*, the dons of a women's college at Oxford University are plagued by a mischief maker who seems to be one of their own run amok, venting evident sexual hostility through writing anonymous letters, ruining manuscripts, and the like. Alarmed, the dons call in Harriet Vane, a graduate of the college who is now a mystery novelist and, not incidentally, the object of

Peter Wimsey's desire. Unable to solve the problem of the Poltergeist/Poison Pen—as one don names her—Harriet calls in Wimsey, who sifts through the information Harriet has collected and identifies the perpetrator in a dramatic, staged demystification that parodies an academic lecture (and that prompts the criminal to confess). Read in a conventional way, *Gaudy Night* seems to conform to the traditional requirements of the genre, with Wimsey functioning as the authoritative central figure who separates the false from the true clues and satisfactorily solves the problem. However, the reader reading consciously as a woman will experience *Gaudy Night* quite differently, perceiving Peter's solution not as satisfactory or complete, but as just another fragment in a puzzle that extends well beyond the boundaries of the text. Peter deals only with one manifestation of a much larger problem; he believes the problem is solved, but Harriet and the woman reader know otherwise. The mystery at the center of *Gaudy Night* is not the mystery of who is responsible for the nocturnal acts of mischief, but of female character and female development in a male-ordered world. The dons of Shrewsbury College represent a violation of social order—they are celibate women, living in a female community, pursuing work of their own—while their tormentor is a male-identified woman, spurred to action by love of a man (her dead husband) and by fear and hatred of the female dons, who seem to her to be unnatural women. The poltergeist, then, embodies conventional definitions of womanhood, with her intrusion into Shrewsbury representing the intrusion of the hostile outside world into the cloister. *Gaudy Night* asks: What are the possible ways for women to live? Can women have both love and work? Is love enough? Is work enough? The novel answers few of the questions it raises, despite Peter's conviction that the puzzle is solved.

Some crime novels teach us how to read as women by focusing on a female detective's thought processes. This is true of many of the Amanda Cross books, but most strikingly and effectively so in *Death in a Tenured Position,* in which Kate Fansler tries to discover the murderer of Janet Mandelbaum, the first woman tenured by Harvard's English Department. As Kate investigates Janet's death, we read Janet from Kate's perspective and Harvard from both Janet's and Kate's, remaining—like the dead woman professor and the living one—always on the outside of the community of male scholars, beyond the ivied walls. This novel forces us to read as the Other, the excluded one, and by doing so helps us to *feel* what killed Janet, a male-identified woman who scorned and mocked the feminist movement. Several reviewers of *Death in a Tenured Position* complained that Cross "cheated" with this book because the murder is no murder after all, but such complaints miss the point, I think: there *is* a murder in this novel, but no one to be brought to justice at the end, just a sense that the whole society in which Janet lived, including Janet herself, is responsible for her death. We are left with disorder, not a restoration of order, at the conclusion of *Death in a Tenured Position;* indeed, the novel suggests that the restoration of order is a false ideal, as the order to which Harvard would like to return is built upon the systematic exclusion of women. It is order, in fact, that killed Janet Mandelbaum. Cross's metaquestion is "who kills women and why?" Her answer, in part, is "the established order."

Then there are writers like Maureen Moore and Barbara Wilson, whose novels, like Cross's, have at their hearts feminist consciousnesses. All three writers take their readers through a process of consciousness raising while their protagonists investigate crimes, with the process of raising one's consciousness a necessary corollary to solving the puzzle presented. Cross's Kate Fansler and Wilson's Pam Nilsen, although in many particulars squarely in the tradition of the amateur detective, differ in one important way from the usual series character: neither functions as an authority figure who finally establishes a single vision of reality. Cross and Wilson allow many voices to speak in their novels and endow their central characters with the great gifts of fallibility and tolerance. Neither Pam nor Kate is able to explain away disorder, nor does either want to; each respects, indeed enjoys, diversity, and each is intensely, personally, aware that what society calls justice may actually be most unjust. The Fansler and Nilsen series enact feminist values, showing subjectivity superior to pretenses of objectivity, involvement more valuable than distance, and compassion more important than justice. The protagonist of Maureen Moore's *Fieldwork* goes Fansler and Nilsen one better: she outright rejects the possibility that an activist women's health group would resort to violence to further their agenda, even though many clues seem to point to one of their number as the murderer of a particularly misogynist doctor. When Marsha Lewis asks herself "who kills to prove a point?" she cannot truthfully answer "feminists." By trusting her understanding of women and holding her own support of other women higher than her desire to solve the crime quickly, Marsha—a graduate student in urban ethnography and, in a nice twist, a supposedly detached observer of a police investigation—is able to discover the real killer and to lead the police to him.

Fieldwork is a feminist fusion of two familiar varieties of the crime novel: the academic mystery and the police procedural. Among writers of crime novels, academe seems a favorite setting—perhaps there is something about academic life that sets both men and women thinking about bloody murder, as many crime writers are professors (like Amanda Cross, aka Carolyn Heilbrun, professor of English at Columbia University), as are many protagonists of crime novels. The academy may be an updated version of the country house of British "Golden Age" detective fiction: a carefully limited setting that presents a finite number of possible suspects, all of whom have motive but none (apparently) opportunity for the killing. From a feminist perspective, the academy functions as a microcosm of the larger world: women academics, no matter their achievements or talents, seem always just outside the real power of the system. Then, too, women entered academe earlier and in larger numbers than they did other such worlds unto themselves—banking, insurance, police forces, etc.—and in training to be scholars learned the investigative skills likely to serve the amateur detective well.[9]

Not all female detectives are academicians, of course; there is quite a range of occupations represented in novels featuring female detectives, and so in the chapters that follow I will be dealing with crime novels according to the type of detective each features, focusing throughout on series characters, with only occasional considerations of single-book detectives. The second chapter, "Free-lancing Amateurs," treats books whose protagonists are not professional detectives, but who investigate crime as a sort of hobby. The third, "Death and the Academy," focuses on novels whose protagonists, like Kate Fansler, are academics who some-how get tangled up in murder with satisfying regularity. The fourth, "New Procedures for Police?" looks at novels featuring female police detectives, while the fifth, "Loners and Hard-Boiled Women," is about female characters who are professional private investigators. The final chapter, "Lesbian Detectives," requires a bit more explanation, for this chapter includes female characters who fit into the categories taken up in earlier chapters, but who are linked by their shared lesbianism. I want to deal with these novels together because the lesbian crime novel is fast becoming a distinctive subgenre, and one that most directly challenges ge-neric conventions by making explicit the social critique that is more covert in most other crime novels. Many lesbian crime nov-els include coming out stories and romances, with the love inter-est frequently taking center stage, shifting the mystery proper to the wings. These novels tend also to make the most extensive and searching use of social criticism, with the crimes they center on often extreme versions of quite ordinary crimes against women or the consequences of such crimes. Valerie Miner's *Murder in the English Department,* for instance, focuses on the death of a notorious sexual harasser, while Wilson's *Sisters of the Road* exam-ines interrelated crimes against women, including child sexual abuse, forced prostitution, and rape. Lesbian crime novels more often than other women's mysteries address issues of race and class as well, illuminating the conjunction of sex, race, and class oppression.

This last points to one obvious lacuna in this book: the absence of black and Asian authors and protagonists. The world of crime fiction is almost exclusively white, with some representation of ethnic and working-class people; despite a great deal of search-ing, I have yet to find a crime novel written by a woman of color and only two series featuring women of color in the position of detective, both written by Marcia Muller. This fact underscores my earlier assertion that the institution of crime fiction is, or at the very least appears to be, fundamentally conservative, uphold-ing ideals and values that members of oppressed groups must find antipathetic to their own lives and struggles. Lesbian writers represent the group farthest from traditional centers of power now found in crime fiction. For now, one must only imagine what a crime novel by a black woman might be like, perhaps using Toni Morrison's *Song of Solomon*—which begins with a seemingly inexplicable suicide and moves through an investigation of a secret society bent on murder—as fuel for one's imagination.

Song of Solomon brings me to the issue of quality, as Morrison's novel, which is not essentially a crime novel, is widely acknowledged to be high art whereas most crime novels are not. The feminist crime novel is still in its youth, and so aesthetic judgments seem premature now. Then, too, I am not primarily (or even secondarily) interested in ranking writers according to some abstract scale of value; however, the fact is that some of the writers I discuss here are both more interesting and more skilled than others. Not all women's crime novels are created equal, and it would be dishonest to pretend they are. In the pages that follow, the judgments I make about literary merit are of course subjective, and I will try to make my standards clear as I go along. Generally speaking, though, attractive ideology cannot substitute for good plotting, skillful characterization, and elegant writing, nor does weak ideology necessarily mar an intriguing puzzle that has other merits. In any case, my hope is that this book will provoke discussion of writers often neglected by critics of crime fiction and that readers will discover new writers whose books will bring them pleasure.

2

Free-lancing Amateurs

The amateur detective, whether male or female, presents problems of logistics and of verisimilitude to the author, and of believability to the reader. Murder, after all, is a fairly infrequent occurrence; the creator of a mystery featuring an amateur sleuth, then, is immediately confronted with the necessity of inventing plausible reasons for the sleuth's entanglement in a murder investigation, while the reader often has to take a larger leap of faith than is comfortable. Such problems are further complicated if the detective features in a series; readers may accept kindly, ordinary Mr. or Ms. X's life being disrupted by *one* murder case, but have a harder time accepting the third or fourth (or tenth or twentieth). Without such acceptance, the mystery cannot be read with much pleasure or involvement. When the detective is a woman, the problems increase geometrically, because the author must then deal in some way with the prevailing conception of women as a group belonging to the private sphere, while the public sphere of action belongs to men. Murder, and particularly the investigation of murder, may begin in the private sphere, but it is by its very nature public, part of the male domain of order and authority. Adrienne Rich sees this dichotomy of female/ private and male/public as a critical feminist issue: "Fundamental to women's oppression is the assumption that we as a group belong to the 'private' sphere of the home, the hearth, the family, the sexual, the emotional, out of which men emerge as adults to act in the 'public' arena of power, the 'real' world, and to which they return for mothering, for access to female forms of intimacy, affection and solace unavailable in the realm of male struggle and competition."[1] The author who creates a female amateur detective, then, is violating traditional gender boundaries, implicitly challenging the dichotomous vision basic to the oppression of women. Some authors attempt to explain away this irruption of the private into the public, undermining the challenge presented to traditional gender-based social arrangements, while others make the implicit challenge explicit, building their plots around the doubled violation of murder and of female involvement in the public work of detection.

Perhaps the best-known female, amateur series detective is also one of the earliest of the genre, Agatha Christie's Miss Marple. Writing at a time when few women worked at jobs that would bring them into contact with *any* members of the public, much less murderous ones, Christie did not have access to recently popular methods of explaining an amateur detective's involvement in crime; she did, however, have available stereotypes of women, and used them to her advantage. Miss Jane Marple, an elderly spinster, is garrulous and nosy, a near caricature of a gossipy old lady; she is also a devoted bird-watcher, a hobby that explains her habit of carrying binoculars around her neck, and an inveterate gardener, which gives a reason for her seeing and hearing everything that goes on in St. Mary Mead and elsewhere. Christie's portrayal of Miss Marple employs and criticizes (by mocking) gender stereotypes. On the one hand, people habitually underestimate Miss Marple's intelligence and the threat she poses to the guilty, allowing themselves to be deceived by appearances—an error Christie's narratives prevent the reader from making for long—and by conventional attitudes toward old, unmarried women. On the other, Miss Marple tends to solve crimes by a combination of intuition and intrusiveness, in marked contrast to the eminently rational methods of Hercule Poirot. Although I would hesitate to call Agatha Christie a feminist, as at least one recent writer has done,[2] there are feminist elements in the Marple novels that deserve notice; the most significant of these is the valorization of precisely those feminine qualities ridiculed in the stereotype of the irrational, intuitive, gossipy spinster. Christie shows the advantages women's ways of thinking may have: Miss Marple's interest in people is not mere nosiness, but evidence of a lifelong study of human nature to which she has brought, and through which she has cultivated, acuity, insight, intelligence, and imagination. Miss Marple invariably sees something about people that others do not, evidencing a shrewdness and an awareness of potential (or realized) evil that does not belie, but explores, her conventionally feminine exterior. Miss Marple's habit of disguising her sharp mind is a conventionally feminine strategy akin to Christie's portrayal of her character as no threat to established social arrangements.

In Eugenia Potter, Virginia Rich has created one of the very few recent detectives in the Miss Marple tradition while bringing some of the latent feminism in Christie's work more sharply into relief. An upper–middle-class widow who divides her time between a ranch in Arizona and a cottage in Maine, Mrs. Potter shares Jane Marple's intense interest in people, her intelligence, and her trust of intuition; she also shares the Marple love of conversation, with her methods of detection parodying a "talking cure" at several points in *The Nantucket Diet Murders* (1985), *The Baked Bean Supper Murders* (1983), and *The Cooking School Murders* (1982), all of which feature detailed descriptions of, and even recipes for, a number of treats and have been favorably reviewed in *Cuisine* and other unexpected places. In *The Baked Bean Supper Murders,* the murderer of four people and of Mrs. Potter's dog turns out to be himself a victim of both his overprotective mother (herself one of his victims and, earlier, a victim of social prejudices against women generally and fat women in particular) and the social class system that Mrs. Potter accepts despite serious reservations. In *The Nantucket Diet Murders,* Rich explores the cultural obsession with thinness and the booming diet industry that obsession supports, while also making points about women's friendships and sense of worth by focusing on eight privileged women who have summered on Nantucket with husbands and children, but most of whom now are widowed and looking for something to do or someone to do nothing with. Unfortunately, Rich misses most of the satirical and political possibilities inherent in such a cast of characters, instead asking the reader to take her characters seriously without giving much thought to the social conditions that created them. Indeed, the novel's concluding chapter even incorporates a series of diet tips that undercut earlier chapters' criticism of the weight-loss industry. Fat, in this novel, is emphatically not a feminist issue, nor are widowhood, aging, sexuality, or female friendship. The Mrs. Potter mysteries are puzzling less for their overt mysteries—all of which are fairly easy to figure out, but which always involve Mrs. Potter's close brush with death before she untangles them—than for the extra-textual mysteries they present: how is it that Virginia Rich consistently chooses topics and situations crying out for analysis, especially feminist analysis, but then fails to analyze them? The failure of imagination here is lamentable, particularly because Mrs. Potter herself is an intriguing character with a complex set of attitudes, including a nascent awareness of the comparative ease of her own background and life circumstances.

One of the odd elements of this series is Mrs. Potter's widowhood. Rich's strategy in creating while dispatching the dead husband, Lew, seems (at least) double—the fact there once was a Lew who is no more both removes Mrs. Potter from the realm of the Marpleish spinster detective and explains, in a culturally acceptable way, her freedom of movement. That is, one need not look on Mrs. Potter as a potentially subversive, single, wholly independent woman, as her "normalcy" is certified by her long marriage to Lew (fondly and frequently recalled in each novel); nevertheless, Mrs. Potter functions as an unencumbered woman, one of the few female amateur detectives to solve crimes independently, without the aid of a male partner. She is also one of the even fewer older female characters who is available for romance, being both unmarried and very clearly sexually alive.

Although a rule laid down by the Detection Club asserts that the detective must not have a romantic interest, as such a subplot might overshadow the puzzle that should be the murder mystery's entire concern,[3] this rule has been more honored in the breach than by the observance; it seems almost mandatory now that crime novels include a love interest, and I notice on the bookstore shelves an entire subgenre called "mystery romances." The combination of courtship and crime investigation can work to enhance a mystery, particularly if the tension inherent in both is exploited. "Mystery romances" are merely the most obvious manifestation of the generally ignored female gothic roots of women's crime novels. Even Dorothy Sayers, one of the founders of the Detection Club and a staunch supporter of its rules, broke the ban on romance in the series of novels featuring Harriet Vane and Peter Wimsey, and in so doing wrote her most complex and abidingly interesting novel, *Gaudy Night.*

Sayers seems to have introduced Harriet—in *Strong Poison,* wherein she is accused of murdering her love, Philip Boyes— mostly as a device to develop Lord Peter Wimsey's character, but by the third novel in which she appears, *Gaudy Night,* Harriet has moved well beyond her initial function. From the beginning, Harriet is a highly unconventional female character: Oxford educated, a mystery writer who earns enough to support herself, sure of her intellectual abilities but far less certain of her emotions, willing to be a social pariah for the sake of her integrity (having lived with Boyes, Harriet refuses to marry him because she objects to the idea of "having matrimony offered as a bad-conduct prize").[4] It is Harriet's unconventionality that makes her the perfect suspect in Boyes's murder, from the legal system's standpoint: such an "unwomanly" woman must be capable of the most heinous acts. Peter, to his credit, does not fall into the trap of stereotypical assumptions; he nevertheless fails to fully comprehend Harriet's character. During the course of three novels— *Strong Poison, Have His Carcase,* and *Gaudy Night*—Harriet teaches Peter what it means to be a woman who rejects traditional definitions of womanhood in a male-ordered world. The Harriet-Peter plot counterpoints the mystery in each of the three novels: while putting together the pieces of the puzzle, Peter must also work at putting together his knowledge of Harriet. Each task requires an open mind, a rejection of biased assumptions, intuition, an ability to listen attentively, and careful examination of details. Ultimately, Peter's success in the mystery is signaled by his identification of the criminal; with Harriet his success is signaled by the terms in which he couches the proposal Harriet accepts— "Placetne, magistra?"—with the Latin and the use of Harriet's university title marking Peter's understanding of the importance of independence and of work to Harriet. In all of the Harriet/ Peter novels, Wimsey remains the important detective, with Harriet playing a subordinate role in the investigations; even in *Gaudy Night,* which centers on Harriet's experiences, it is Peter who finally solves the mystery.

Following a similar pattern are the Maggie Rome series by Lucille Kallen and the Sarah Deane series by J. S. Borthwick, with the latter incorporating a romance parallel to the Wimsey-Vane relationship in Sayers's novels. Borthwick introduced Sarah Deane in *The Case of the Hook-Billed Kites* (1982), in which Sarah, a Boston University graduate student and English teacher, is briefly suspected of murdering her almost-lover, Philip Lentz— with the dead man's name a nod to Sayers's Harriet Vane and the situation, murder on a bird-watching excursion in Texas, a nod to Christie's Miss Marple.[5] Although the *Kites* book jacket identifies Sarah as the "delightful and intrepid amateur detective" and the novel opens in Sarah's consciousness, the narrative rapidly shifts its focus to Alex McKenzie, a bird-watching doctor and friend of Philip's who is in Texas to investigate the importation of a bogus cancer cure from Mexico. *Kites,* Borthwick's first novel, exhibits many of the predictable flaws of first books: too many obvious clues scattered about, too many dimly defined characters, confusion in point of view, and awkward narrative shifts. Most significant among these flaws is Borthwick's evident inability to decide who is the main character, Sarah or Alex. Much of the novel chronicles Alex's deepening attachment to Sarah and her emotional uncertainty. Unlike Harriet Vane, whose perception of the social opposition between love and work forms a barrier to her relationship with Peter Wimsey, Sarah sees no love/work dichotomy—perhaps a statement about the differing social conditions for women in 1934 and 1982—but does worry about her desire for dependence, admitting late in the novel that she was involved with Philip "for the wrong reasons. I was looking for someone to make the world safe" (p. 197).

The problems that make *Kites* fall short as a mystery, including the shift of the detective's role from Sarah to Alex, actually contribute to the novel's richness, if looked at from a slightly different perspective. Ostensibly concerned with crime, on a deeper level *Kites* is about a young woman's psychological coming of age, with Philip's murder marking a division between the child Sarah and the woman Sarah. The female Bildungsroman in the nineteenth and early twentieth centuries often culminates in the heroine's engagement or marriage,[6] reflecting social conditions proscribing other alternatives for adult women. In the later part of the twentieth century, however there is a move away from this pattern. Now female Bildungsromane often end in ways similar to the male versions, with the (female) hero's assumption of a role in the wider world[7] challenging the private/public dichotomy. *Kites* follows the latter pattern, with Sarah's maturation compressed into just a few days.

Three moments of self-recognition and pain illuminate Sarah's journey; significantly, during the first of these moments Sarah is gazing into a mirror, in which she sees an alien version of herself. Two days after Philip's body is found, Sarah sees "some thin, pale stranger reflected [in the mirror], eyes charcoal smudges in a taut face" (p. 75). As she looks at "this stranger, alone, unimportant":

Suddenly, Sarah was overwhelmed by an ache from within so acute that she almost cried out. She wanted to go home, really home. Not to that garage apartment in Boston, but to the first one—that faded brick house that stood at the front of the long spruce-lined driveway. Home. . . .

. . . An overwhelming sense of loss swept Sarah. She stood bereft in the middle of the motel room staring into a mirror. . . . Home, house vanished. Naomi [her cat] was dead, run over. Sneezer [her dog] was gone, shot by a deerhunter. The house sold, her father and mother moved from New Hampshire to a series of strange houses holding only guest rooms for grown and gone-away children. Tony in Vermont selling skis, her little brother over six feet tall with a black beard. Tears ran down her face and along her nose into her mouth, and she licked her lips and tasted salt. (pp. 76–77)

Sarah's desire for home only briefly masks her deeper wish to return to childhood, to a seemingly less complicated relation between self and world. Sarah moves out of the motel the next day, at least partly to escape the mirror (and, symbolically, herself), after beginning a reconstruction of her childhood by acquiring both a substitute dog and a substitute mother.[8] The move from the motel represents a second break with the mother, though, as Sarah trades her newly found surrogate mother (or recovered mother) for the more acceptable mother substitute in an adult woman's life, a man. The same day that she moves, Sarah forces herself to "sort things out," deciding that her "whole life seemed to have been tending from muddle to muddle for a long time, and now she was at the center of a monster one" (pp. 126–27).

The second illuminating moment occurs as Sarah tries to sort through this "muddle," and the reader sees that Sarah's progress toward adulthood has been marked by three violent deaths—her dog's, Philip's, and an earlier boyfriend's—each a literal enactment of the symbolic death of Sarah's preoedipal relationship with her mother, as each death has pushed her further from childhood and home, out into the (masculine) world of work and of heterosexual attachment. Sarah doesn't recognize this link among the deaths, although she does feel there must be a connection, at one point musing about the possible meaning of the letter *P*, which began both men's names and the name she has chosen for her new dog.

The final, and most important, moment of painful self-recognition occurs three days later, when Sarah likens herself to Dorothy in the Oz books:

She saw that all her life she had believed, like Dorothy, that someone would turn up and do things for her, or with her, while she played at being the liberated woman. Her whole life had been made by protective screens, loving parents, Miss Morton's boarding school. And at college, when she was adrift for the first time, Pres [her first lover, now dead] had turned up and they had played house together. And when she lost Pres— why, there was Philip ready to take charge of her life. . . .

. . . And look at Alex McKenzie, right on deck as doctor-nursemaid, so that great big Sarah can go on living in Oz. (p. 181)

At this point, Sarah realizes that she needs to draw back from involvement with Alex if she is ever fully to know herself. As the novel ends, with Philip's murder solved and a third potential victim saved by Alex and Sarah, Sarah returns to Boston, promising to call Alex when she feels ready.

The murder mystery and the tracing of Sarah's maturation in *Kites* are essentially separate narratives, with her development contributing little to the solution of the puzzle and vice versa. There is even a certain dissonance between the two plots, as the murder turns out to have been quite traditional (a man killed by another man for reasons of greed and self-protection); the reader's understanding of Sarah and of the particularly female psychological issues she confronts proves to be unrelated to the mystery. In other words, the mystery of (female) character and the mystery of whodunit are at odds. In the second Borthwick murder mystery, *The Down East Murders* (1985), issues of female psychology are more vitally related to the central plot and are worked out in more subtle and sophisticated ways than is true in *Kites*. This novel finds Sarah and Alex in coastal Maine, where Sarah is working at a small museum for the summer and Alex is visiting his mother, a well-known artist. A series of art thefts, the suspicious "accidental" drowning of an elderly couple, and the murder of an ill-natured local artist draw the two into a second investigation. This time, though, it is Sarah who solves the crimes, thereby nearly causing her own death—a device too frequently employed in novels featuring female detectives—but saving the life of Alex's cousin Giddy, whose name reflects one part of her personality. The art thefts and the drowning are only tangentially connected to the murder, which was committed by the victim's wife.

The portraits of several women, including the murderer, are the greatest strengths of this novel. Abused by her husband for years, Marian Harwood is pushed into leaving him by Elspeth McKenzie, Alex's independent and very strong mother, who also arranges a "raid" on the Harwood house to take away Marian's furniture. When Nate's body is discovered later, no one suspects Marian of the crime, especially when her son Roger, who actually witnessed the murder, falsely confesses. As the police investigator says later, "Roger says his father didn't even try to defend himself. . . . Nate just turned and stared, little mouse Marian coming at him with a doorstop. She'd probably never so much as lifted a spoon to him all those years. Roger, too. He just stood there and didn't believe it" (p. 290). Elspeth McKenzie, like the others, decides that Marian simply snapped from years of ill treatment: "Always such a mouse, such a doormat. Never a raised voice. Not until she walked out on Nate. I suppose that's it. She just burst out and began *doing* things" (p. 288). The easy assumptions people make about women based on gender stereotypes are overturned in the novel's final chapters, as the reader learns that Marian was not just a "doormat," that the investigation would have moved faster had not a male detective assumed a female deputy was hasty (p. 290), and that key evidence was obtained with the medical advice of a nurse Alex had assumed was merely a pretty featherbrain. In a perhaps predictable development, Sarah feels sure enough of herself by the end of this novel to allow her relationship with Alex to move toward sexual involvement.

The solution to part of the mystery in *Down East* curiously parallels Borthwick's handling of one theme in the novel. Sarah discovers that the art thief has hidden the pictures behind Impressionist prints; she is led to this discovery by the absence of the usual hardware—wire, hooks, etc.—on the back of the framed prints. Significantly, the first stolen artwork Sarah finds, by stripping away the paper backing, is a painting by Elspeth McKenzie: what Sarah finds, then, is the work of a mother that has been "papered over," hidden, with the work of a man (Renoir) by a man (Sydney Prior). Similarly, the theme of mothers and mothering in *Down East* is a covert or a buried one, imperfectly hidden behind the overt themes of death and heterosexual love. We know from *Kites* that Sarah feels motherless but has in the past chosen men to take a mother's place with her; in *Down East,* Sara accepts Alex as a lover only after she gets to know his mother, in a development that suggests Sarah chooses Alex as a way to have his mother become her own mother. Elspeth is a particularly attractive mother figure for Sarah, as the older woman is a dedicated artist, a believer in women's rights, and an intelligent, independent woman who has never accepted conventional definitions of motherhood or of womanhood. Marian Harwood's history further develops this theme, as Marian is Elspeth's opposite, a conventional, passive woman wholly dedicated to husband and son until she "breaks out," in Elspeth's terms, killing her husband, attacking her son, and allowing that son to accept the blame for his father's death. Marian, then, seems to be a warning about the dangers of repression and of oppression; she is also the "bad mother," who takes life instead of giving it, who destroys instead of nurturing, and therefore embodies Sarah's fears and uncertainties.

The covert theme of motherhood in *Down East* can help to illustrate the ways in which a feminist might revise Geraldine Pederson-Krag's now-classic "Detective Stories and the Primal Scene." Pederson-Krag, applying Freudian theory to detective fiction, argues that the "intense curiosity" aroused by the detective story is rooted in its association with the primal scene—the child's first observation or imagined observation of sexual intercourse between his or her parents—with the crime corresponding to the sexual act, the victim representing the parent for whom the child has negative oedipal feelings, and the detective (and the reader) standing in for the child.[9] Using this formulation, Nate Harwood would represent Sarah's mother, which seems a grossly simplified and distorting reading of the novel, particularly in view of the novel's thematic use of actual and symbolic mothers. Nancy Chodorow's argument about the differences between male and female development can be used to construct an alternative reading of this text. Chodorow argues that girls form their identities through connectedness and similarities to the mother, while boys seek separation and difference. Typically, then, women may have difficulty with individuation and with separation.[10] If we apply this formulation to *Down East,* what we see is a symbolic enactment not of the primal scene—at least not for Sarah, nor for the female reader—but of the entry into adulthood, in which the world of the fathers, represented here by Nate Harwood and Sidney Prior, presents a threat to the emerging adult woman[11] that can be overcome either through a violent rejection, which is both terrifying and unacceptable, or through an identification with a mother who both nurtures *and* acts independently in the world. The dangers of total merger with the mother are worked out through the character of Marian Harwood, whose foray into violence is part of her own regression into a childlike state.[12]

Elspeth McKenzie offers Sarah an appealing alternative to immersion in the patriarchal world or to merger with the mother, serving as a model of adult womanhood that includes love, self-esteem, independence, and meaningful, creative work. The psychological concerns in *Down East* are tightly interwoven with the murder mystery itself, making this novel more sophisticated and interesting than Borthwick's first book, *Kites*; nevertheless, neither of the Borthwick novels is really compelling, primarily because Sarah is too simple a character, from whom the reader feels a certain distance.

The desire to bridge that distance may be a component of many authors' choice of first-person narrator, the point of view taken in Anne Morice's Tessa Crichton, Barbara Paul's Geraldine Ferrar, Marcia Muller's Elena Oliverez, and Lucille Kallen's Maggie Rome/C. B. Greenfield series. The Crichton and Ferrar series are fun but strictly light entertainment, and not of particular feminist interest. Ferrar, of course was an actual Metropolitan Opera soprano at the time of Caruso and Toscanini, and Paul, who has obviously done a tremendous job of research for this series, has good fun bringing Ferrar and other Met stars back to life in a series of fictitious adventures.[13] Morice's Tessa Crichton is a British actress married to a Scotland Yard chief inspector. Tessa's public career explains the large circle of acquaintances and the travel necessary to run into murder so frequently as she does, while her husband's profession and her own growing fame as an amateur detective help to explain the consistency with which members of that circle ask her assistance in solving crimes.[14] Neither Paul nor Morice seems much interested in developing or deepening her detective's character, as both Tessa and Geraldine remain fairly static characters from novel to novel, neither changing in response to the murders investigated.

Kallen's Maggie Rome, in contrast, begins the series as a sort of Watson to C. B. Greenfield's Holmes or Archie to his Nero Wolfe, but in later books moves to a more prominent position. Reading the books featuring Maggie Rome in sequential order reveals Kallen's interest moving away from the nearly perfect, rational C. B. Greenfield to the imperfect, conflicted Maggie Rome. The first novel in the series, *Introducing C. B. Greenfield* (1979), sets up the terms of the Greenfield/Rome relationship and establishes their situation: fiftyish Greenfield is the publisher of the *Sloan's Ford Reporter,* a Westchester village weekly for which Maggie, forty or so, is a reporter. Greenfield and Maggie also share an interest in classical music, but otherwise their personal lives seldom overlap, with Maggie knowing little about how Greenfield, a widower with two grown daughters, spends his time and Greenfield caring little about how Maggie, who is married to a businessman and has two near-adult sons, spends hers. In their first investigation, Maggie does most of the legwork by Greenfield's direction, while he does much of the thinking. Maggie chafes against the restrictions imposed by Greenfield, and by the ways in which her relationship with him conflicts with her own self-assessment and with her general principles. From the first, Maggie is a sort of practical feminist; that is, the conditions of her life and her own intelligence have led her to feminist positions without her actually considering the theoretical basis of those positions. By way of example, in the second book in the series, *The Tanglewood Murder* (1980), Maggie and Greenfield meet a woman who appears to rely on the kindness of male strangers, about whom Maggie muses, "There was some archaic kind of femininity about Eleanor Springer, something that belonged to an earlier cultural pattern. She reminded me of a pampered showdog who has lost its master on Fifth Avenue and is elegantly and distractedly dodging traffic because it hasn't the sense to know why the red and green lights are there" (p. 27). Maggie admires women who are strong and self-sufficient, like Victoria Hollis of *Introducing* and like herself.

Despite the conventionally hierarchical relationship of male and female main characters in the first few Rome/Greenfield books, the plots themselves raise interesting questions about gender and about social class. In *Introducing,* for instance, the villain is a self-centered male writer who mistreats women, robbing his wife of the confidence she should rightfully have in her own considerable talent as a photographer; his crime—hitting a twelve-year-old boy with his car and then fleeing the scene—is consistent with his personality. The women Maggie gets to know during the course of this investigation include Sidonie Seberg, a young publishing executive whom Kallen may have created expressly to critique an unpleasant byproduct of the contemporary feminist movement. Sidonie has seized the opportunities opened by feminism to advance in a career, but has not otherwise embraced feminist positions; indeed, her life seems an egotistical distortion of such positions, as she takes on a masculine role that approximates the villain's: she ignores her young daughter, dedicates herself entirely to success as traditionally defined for men, has no women friends, and carries on an affair with a married man without concern for his wife or daughter.

As if fearful that her contemptuous description of Sidonie Seberg in *Introducing* might be construed as a criticism of the fruits of the women's movement, in her third novel, *No Lady in the House* (1982), Kallen examines the broad social changes brought about by women's increasing freedom. Sloan's Ford, a bedroom community from which the men originally commuted to jobs in the city while the women stayed home to care for children, is now almost deserted during the day, the women all having found jobs. Although Maggie and Greenfield are generally on the side of old ways against new—both hate rock music, despise yuppies, are deeply suspicious of technology, and wistfully remember what seemed a simpler time—the one change Maggie strongly favors is the dismantling of the feminine mystique. However, Kallen is also aware of the limitations of women's freedom: not all women can have careers—the very word implies middle-class education and opportunity—and many have always had jobs, not from a desire for self-fulfillment but because they had to work to survive. In *No Lady*, Maggie's increasing awareness of class difference serves as a prompt to the reader to raise her (or his) consciousness at the same time, as her investigation teaches her about the minority, working-class women who come to Sloan's Ford each day to perform the domestic chores their wealthier sisters have escaped.

By the fifth Greenfield/Rome novel, *A Little Madness* (1986), Maggie has decided to get involved with the women's peace movement, joining a women's encampment to protest a missile base in upstate New York. This decision has less than pure motives, as Maggie has begun to feel jealous about Greenfield, despite having earlier described their relationship as "consisting of equal parts of comfortable friendship, grudging respect, and simple exasperation" (*Tanglewood*, p. 19), and now feels that need to escape: "I needed air. I need to breathe deeply, to act, do something simple, direct, useful. Preferably where there were no men to worry about. No men to appease, to impress, to satisfy, to contend with, to compete for, to rely on, to be betrayed by, to entertain, to seduce, love, loathe, *care* about" (*Madness*, p. 29). Nevertheless, Maggie becomes deeply committed both to the peace camp and to the individual women in it. In *Madness*, after a right-wing woman modeled closely on Phyllis Schlafly is murdered, a piece of evidence incriminating a member of the women's peace camp is found, but Maggie discovers the real killer, exonerating the protestors. Alice Dakin, the victim, is a totally unlikable but very powerful woman:

A crusader, out to save the country from a long list of undesirables that included peace activists, feminists, intellectuals, union members, homosexuals, students from the more advanced universities, supporters of Medicare, civil rights and school lunches, aliens, environmentalists, all those in favor of banning handguns, and anyone suspected of being an unregenerate Democrat. With the Bible in one hand, a hair dryer in the other, and her eye firmly fixed on national prominence, Alice Dakin rode fearlessly at the head of a small but loyal army, a sort of Joan of Arc of prejudice. (p. 37)

The murderer, one of that loyal army, is far more sympathetic than is the victim. Maggie learns that the murder was accidental, done by an overwrought, highly traditional woman who saw her life coming apart and concocted a desperate plot to fix it: she wanted to arrange a fake kidnapping, cast suspicion on the women's peace camp, and remove (by having arrested) her husband's lover, a member of the camp. Alice Dakin rejects the plot, however, saying she "couldn't be party to anything like that" (p. 206). The distraught woman, convinced her plot is "the only way to save my life. . . . What would I do where would I go," picks up a pillow and smothers Alice, "just want[ing] her to stay in the *room*" (pp. 206–7). The working out of the puzzle in *Madness* offers twinned observations: that women, right-wing or feminist, are unlikely to kill at all, but if they do their motives are more likely to be deeply personal than entirely political, with personal and political linked inextricably. The political commitments of the women in *Madness* are honorable ones—even Alice Dakin is principled enough to refuse immoral tactics—and the novel asks that we honor those commitments.

The narrative voice of the Greenfield/Rome books is the series's particular attraction. Maggie's sense of humor and her absolute honesty draw the reader into the books. Greenfield, the genius detective, is infinitely less interesting than is Maggie, despite Kallen's attempts to deepen him by revealing unexpected facets of his character in each novel. Greenfield doesn't seem to learn anything new about himself or others through his investigations, whereas Maggie changes and grows with each experience. Too often the Greenfield/Rome relationship takes on a father/child configuration, with Greenfield as a godlike figure who sees all and knows all and Maggie the wondering, admiring apprentice. Greenfield's relative fixity and Maggie's greater flexibility at times approach a parody of recent feminist personality theory, with the masculine identity more fixed and unitary than the feminine, which changes in response to change and has less rigid boundaries.[15] Maggie's husband and children impinge so little on her consciousness that it's hard to see why Kallen invented them at all, except perhaps for reasons akin to Rich's endowing Eugenia Potter with a now-dead husband: the husband and sons certify Maggie's normalcy, her ordinariness, while also providing a barrier to sexual involvement with Greenfield.

My personal favorite among the amateur female detectives is Marcia Muller's Elena Oliverez, of *The Tree of Death* (1983), *The Legend of the Slain Soldiers* (1985), and *Beyond the Grave* (1986), the last cowritten with Bill Pronzini. Muller, also the author of the Sharon McCone series to be discussed in the fifth chapter, combines some unusual elements in these novels. Not only is the detective a woman, but she is also Chicana, one of only two female minority detectives I have come across in a great deal of mystery reading. Minority characters are scarce in murder mysteries: Rich has a black couple, servants to one of the main characters, in *Nantucket;* Borthwick's *Kites* includes two Chicano characters, one a police detective and one the director of a wildlife refuge; and

Kallen's series has a black couple in minor but recurring roles. For the most part, these minority characters provide the (white) author, narrator, and/or other characters with the opportunity to display their liberalism or with the occasion for comments on others' racism. I suppose these authors' acknowledgment of the existence of nonwhite people is better than the creation of entirely white fictional universes, but it is only marginally better. Muller, in contrast, sets the Oliverez novels almost entirely within the Mexican-American community of Santa Barbara, with Elena's cultural and ethnic heritage a central fact of her character and of the crimes she investigates. Elena resents those who see her ethnicity as "something to be ignored or even forgiven," because "in the last couple of years I'd come to identify more and more with my heritage and my own people. It hadn't always been that way—I'd had more than my share of Anglo friends and a penchant for Anglo boyfriends—but recently that was changing. Maybe it was working at the museum [of Mexican Arts]; maybe it was simply coming of age" (*Soldiers,* p. 41). Most refreshingly, the reader also gets a look at cross-cultural relationships from a perspective seldom encountered in popular culture, as Elena finds herself attracted to a police detective and considers whether she should allow herself to become involved with an Anglo.

More than one critic has remarked on the astonishing literariness of characters in detective fiction—in the novels mentioned thus far in this chapter, both Kallen's and Borthwick's characters have a penchant for the literary allusion or even the spontaneous quotation—but little attention has been paid to the role of the musical and visual arts, both of which feature prominently in mysteries. The solutions to the mysteries in both Oliverez novels, like that in Borthwick's *Down East,* require some knowledge of art on the part of the detective, and Muller incorporates a sort of minicourse on Mexican-American art and history into her novels. As *The Tree of Death* begins, Elena has recently been named curator of the Museum of Mexican Arts, which is about to open in new quarters. By the end of the book, Elena is the director of the museum, having solved the murder of the original director. Muller does an admirable job of interweaving Elena's vocation and her avocation, while simultaneously planting clues to the mystery, sketching out Mexican-American culture and traditions, and deepening Elena's character, delicately balancing all the elements of the novel right to its closing pages. Muller gives Elena a background that enriches one's understanding of and regard for her, providing her with a free-spirited, proud mother who did domestic work to send her daughters to college (Elena has a sister who is a professor at the University of Minnesota) and who is now happily retired to a mostly Mexican-American trailer park, where the murder in *Soldiers* takes place. That Elena now lives in the house where her mother raised her is a revealing detail, typical of Muller's light but sure touch: metaphorically, Elena has chosen to follow her mother's path. The mutual regard of mother and daughter, despite their differences, plays an important role in the novels.

Muller's Oliverez series is feminist in the deepest sense of the term. Women are at the center of the world she creates, with relationships between women seen as basic to every woman's life and women portrayed in all their realistic variety. Muller seems very sensitive to differences among women—differences of age, race, class, ethnicity, personal circumstances—and the first two Oliverez novels celebrate those differences, that variety. The killers in both novels are women, and their victims are men, which may seem both unrealistic and unfeminist—women are far more likely to be victims than murderers—but the motives offered in each instance make psychological sense. Each killer is an idealist who acts on a mistaken conception of honor: Isabel, in *Tree*, kills the museum's director in a fury at his betrayal of the museum she loves through running a lucrative smuggling business in Central American artifacts, while the murderer in *Soldiers* kills first when she believes her lover to have betrayed both her and the labor movement and forty years later when she realizes that the first murder is about to be revealed by a historian. The former of these is a patriarchal woman, who has always deferred to male authority—rather like the female killers in *Kites* and *Madness*—and Elena thinks that the museum director "finally did something that caused all her [the murderer's] repressed rage to boil over" (p. 231). The murderer in *Soldiers*, in contrast, is "a strong-willed woman. . . . Fiery-tempered and as active in the labor movement as [the two male leaders] . . . [she] was extremely free-thinking for a woman of those times [1940s], and she'd had a number of lovers" (p. 168).

The only really discordant note in the first two Oliverez books comes in their conventional endings, in which the killer is captured, order is restored, and Elena draws closer to the Anglo police lieutenant, Dave Kirk. Given Elena's status as a minority woman who is intensely aware of social injustice, it seems odd that she trusts the official system of justice so freely, aiding the police in their inquiries and evidently satisfied that a trial will conclude each case. Muller explains Elena's attitude in *Tree* by making her the police's prime suspect and having her embark on an investigation as a way of saving herself, and, less successfully, in *Soldiers* by making the (second) victim her mother's good friend and having her mother initiate the investigation, as she does not believe the police will find the culprit. Nevertheless, taking a nontraditional detective and a nontraditional criminal and then ending their stories in a completely conventional way strikes me as less satisfying than other possibilities.[16]

Susan Dunlap, like Muller also the author of two mystery series,[17] plays with possible outcomes of investigations in her three Vejay Haskell novels, *An Equal Opportunity Death* (1984), *The Bohemian Connection* (1985), and *The Last Annual Slugfest* (1986), ending only the latest book in the series with the killer turned over to official authority and evidently headed for trial and punishment. The novel with the most conventional solution also posits the most conventional relationship among investigator, victim, and killer, with all Vejay's—and the reader's—sympathies reserved for the victim, leaving little room for identification with the killer. In contrast, the first and second novels in the Haskell series demand empathy with both victims and killers, allowing the killers to speak directly and movingly of the forces that pushed them to murder and detailing Vejay's conflicted responses to her success in solving these puzzles. In *An Equal Opportunity Death*, Vejay regrets having solved the mystery because her solution both destroys the family that welcomed her to the town of Henderson and also casts her out of the community. At the moment when she puts all the pieces of the puzzle together, Vejay thinks, "I knew who the killer was. It only made me feel sad. Had I thought about it before, I would have realized there was no way not to be distressed, no matter who the killer was. My discovery would ruin our community. . . . I wished I could forget about [the victim] and let the murderer go. But I, of all people, had no choice [because she is the sheriff's prime suspect]" (p. 174).

In making Vejay undertake this investigation to save herself from arrest, Dunlap employs a device identical to Muller's in the first Oliverez novel and similar to the explanation offered in many other novels featuring amateur detectives. Vejay's success in this first investigation leads directly to the other investigations, again following a familiar pattern: an acquaintance asks for Vejay's help in *The Bohemian Connection,* citing Vejay's prior experience (pp. 6–8), while Vejay undertakes a murder investigation in *The Last Annual Slugfest* in order to make reparations to the family she hurt by solving her first case.

In contrast to Muller's Elena Oliverez, Vejay Haskell is downwardly mobile, having forsaken a lucrative career as an account executive in San Francisco and divorced her husband in order to live alone in the tiny resort town of Henderson, working as a meter reader for the local branch of Pacific Gas and Electric. The meter-reading job makes Vejay privy to a surprising number of secrets, with electricity usage even providing the vital clue to the puzzle's solution in *An Equal Opportunity Death.* Dunlap brings in several liberal issues as minor themes in her three Haskell novels—land conservation and Native American rights in *The Last Annual Slugfest,* for instance, and all-male, powerful clubs in *The Bohemian Connection*—but the most emotionally resonant theme in all three novels is the theme of families, whether chosen or biological. In both *An Equal Opportunity Death* and *The Last Annual Slugfest,* this theme centers on the Fortigmilios, with Rosa Fortigmilio serving as a substitute mother for Vejay. Rosa is an attractive sort of earth mother, usually portrayed serving up huge dinners for assorted relatives and friends, the very picture of all-nurturing, ideal motherhood. Significantly, though, this all-loving mother withdraws her love from Vejay in *An Equal Opportunity Death;* the last line of the novel describes Rosa's response to Vejay's look: "She turned away" (p. 184). There are conditions to be met before Vejay can regain this love, conditions she meets more than a year later by exonerating Rosa's son of suspicion of murder in *The Last Annual Slugfest*, a book that ends with Rosa and Vejay tearfully hugging. This pattern of the mother's withdrawal of love followed by the daughter's attempt to regain that love or recognition that she can never meet the mother's conditions is familiar from other recent, noncrime novels by women,[18] but in those novels—most notably Alice Walker's *Meridian*—the pattern generally serves as a way of opening up the whole question of definitions of motherhood and the way in which patriarchal constructions of motherhood set mother and daughter in an adversarial relationship.[19] In these two novels, there is no overt critique of motherhood; indeed, there seems total acceptance of Rosa as an ideal mother by conventional standards, with much of the emotional force of both books coming from Vejay's deep desire to reconstitute a preoedipal relation with the mother. Nevertheless, the covert criticism of Rosa has great power: she is always seen surrounded by men, serving men and in turn protected by men, in her warm, womblike kitchen, while Vejay is cast out— quite literally—into the stormy cold. A patriarchal woman, Rosa's first allegiance is to men, with women running a very poor second. Although Vejay deeply regrets discovering Rosa's husband is the murderer in *An Equal Opportunity Death*, this solution is symbolically satisfying: through discovering Carlo's secret, Vejay separates the father and the mother, perhaps hoping she can then step into the gap his absence will create. The last moment of the book, however, shows her defeat: Rosa has substituted a son for the husband, and has literally turned away from Vejay. The symbolism of this novel's conclusion is complicated by Carlo's response to discovery. Trapped in a flooding building, Carlo chooses to save Vejay from the water, knowing that saving her means his own arrest, and then allows himself to be pulled down by the waters. The father here seems willing to give up his place to the daughter, sacrificing himself for her.

The second Vejay Haskell novel deromanticizes father/ daughter relationships, as if revising *An Equal Opportunity Death*'s construction of the father/mother/child triangle. *The Bohemian Connection*'s solution turns on the damaging effects of patriarchally ordered families. The murderer—a woman who killed her brother and then, years later, killed a female neighbor to avoid revelation of the first murder—speaks movingly and at length of her adolescence, spent in service to a mother "too crazy to be left alone" because the father believes "it would have looked bad if people had seen how crazy she was; it would have damaged the business. People don't want to buy a house from a crazy woman's husband" (pp. 175–76). While her brother is free to do as he pleases, the dutiful daughter must give up friends, fun, even her artwork to care for her mother. The son escapes all family responsibilities, yet when the father dies he leaves everything to that son, including the house the daughter lives in and the business her husband has made thrive, because "Daddy loved Ross, only Ross. Ross was his *son*. He always forgave Ross" (p. 176). The inequitable treatment of sons and daughters drives this woman into murderous rage; she tells Vejay she does not regret killing her brother: "I liked killing Ross" (p. 176). Jenny kills her brother in order to keep a room of her own and the money that enables her to paint instead of working at a regular job, as Ross's plans for his inheritance would take both away from her (p. 177). The broader social application of the feminist critique of family arrangements in *The Bohemian Connection* is obvious, as is the implicit warning: present social conditions drive women to madness by requiring women's self-abnegation and service to a patriarchal system that rewards men merely for existing while depriving women of power, property, and meaningful work. This particular daughter's rebellion, prompted by imminent homelessness, against the man who represents her disenfranchisement is a turning outward of the fury that her mother directed inward (she drowned when she escaped confinement). The insane mother echoes the madwoman in the attic of Charlotte Brontë's *Jane Eyre*, and all those other confined, crazy women that haunt the pages of women's novels.[20] Her story, which is only hinted at, and her daughter's, which is more detailed, call into question the ability of the official system of justice—represented in the Haskell novels by a gruff but fair-minded sheriff—to deal with the crimes Vejay has uncovered, since only the daughter's actions are perceived as criminal under the law, while the father's and son's crimes have legal sanction. Similarly, the men of the Bohemian Grove club who cavort in Henderson for a week each year have no fear of legal reprisals—they *are* the legal system, "too big to be bothered by these nuisances" (p. 108)—yet the prostitutes they bring to town *do* fear the law. In a misdirection of female anger, Henderson women form an "anti-hookers group" (p. 7) to harass the female prostitutes, leaving the men untouched "to put on skits in drag, get drunk, and pee in the bushes" (p. 4) but also to hear speeches by major political leaders (also men, of course) (p. 5).

Dunlap's admission of the voice of the murderer into her concluding chapters in all but *The Last Annual Slugfest,* where the killer's speech is reported instead of represented in dialogue, is an implicitly feminist strategy employed also in Muller's Oliverez novels, Kallen's Rome/Greenfield series, and Borthwick's Deane novels. These chapters are written in dialogic fashion, with multiple, distinct voices contributing to the closing—or refusal to close—of the mystery. The characters who participate in these discussions seldom share a unitary point of view, as the depiction of a divided community in the final chapter of *An Equal Opportunity Death* most strikingly illustrates, and there is always at least one character to express compassion for the criminal. In no case is the criminal simply cast out of an order that then restores itself. Muller's, Kallen's, and Dunlap's choice of first-person narrator generally leads them to allow their protagonist/narrator's voices to be the ones last heard, yet none of the three is presented as the unquestionable authority; it is possible to reject these detectives' views of events and to choose instead the versions offered by other characters, or even to read in an individual interpretation. Like Dunlap, Kallen in two novels allows the criminal to speak directly, but in neither case is there a conventional confession, as in Rich's *The Nantucket Diet Murders,* for instance, where the killer tells all in a horrifyingly cold way preparatory to trying to murder Mrs. Potter. Traditional confessions keep the reader at a distance, while Kallen's and Dunlap's shared strategy prompts identification with the criminal by creating an atmosphere for the confession that is free of fear and of tension. In *The Tanglewood Murder,* for example, the murderer speaks passionately of his childhood, with his personal history making clear his motives for murder and the unlikelihood that he would ever kill again. Significantly,

Maggie helps to hide this man's identity and whereabouts from the police even before she hears his story, a choice that indicates an awareness that official justice in some cases may well be unjust. In *A Little Madness,* the reader is given an astonishing stream-of-consciousness anticonfession that evokes compassion for the criminal from the detectives and from the reader, and that also seems calculated to begin a questioning of the reader's own guilty conscience by revealing the inner torment of a person who previously seemed dismissable—a silly woman on the lunatic fringe. Admitting multiple points of view without establishing a hierarchical relationship among them allows the reader an equality with the detective (and with the criminal) missing in masculinist narratives.

3

Death and the Academy

Judging from the number of crime novels set in academe, murder—committing it or investigating it—would seem to rank just behind research and teaching in the list of professorial activities. Male authors who choose academic settings for their novels tend to take a dim view of the academy, focusing on the venality and obtuseness of academics, their love of their own voices, and their inability to see beyond their own pet topics. Perhaps the most entertaining mystery in this subgenre is Robert Barnard's *Death of an Old Goat,* wherein the "old goat" of the title—who gives a memorably bizarre lecture on novelists, mixing up his notes and confusing Jane Austen with Elizabeth Gaskell—is murdered during a lecture tour in Australia. Barnard has great fun mocking Australians, academics, students, third-rate universities, and much else while working toward a solution to the mystery. Women novelists and their female protagonists generally view the academy less negatively, seeing it as potentially better than most institutions while also remaining aware of the ways in which it falls short of its ideals. The protagonist's view of the academy in several novels seems to reflect the female authors'; it is those novels with which I deal in this chapter. Although there are many other crime novels that make use of academe in some fashion—for instance, J. S. Borthwick's Sarah Deane, discussed in the preceding chapter, is an English teacher and graduate student and Elizabeth Peters's Jacqueline Kirby is a college

42

librarian—the ones I discuss in this chapter tend to place academe at the center of their concerns, even though not all of the novels are actually set on college campuses; not included in this discussion are novels, like the Deane and Kirby series, in which the protagonist's (academic) profession is tangential to the plot. Curiously, most female academics/detectives are English professors, which may simply reflect their creators' expertise, but which also places the novels in which they appear in the tradition of the literary crime novel, with literary allusions and quotes sprinkled liberally across their pages.[1] The only female academics/detectives I have found who are *not* English professors are not professors at all, but students, with Victoria Silver's Lauren Adler a case in point.

Silver may be embarking on an Ivy League/Seven Sisters series, as the titles of her first two mysteries suggest: *Death of a Harvard Freshman* (1984) and *Death of a Radcliffe Roommate* (1986).[2] Both books feature Lauren Adler, a Harvard student, as the detective, and both straddle the young-adult and adult markets, saying quite a bit about what it's like to be an eighteen- or nineteen-year-old woman at a prestigious university in the 1980s. Silver, who graduated from Radcliffe, sometimes seems more intrigued with the details of life at Harvard and Radcliffe than she is with carefully constructing a crime plot, but the novels have so much else of interest that the minor flaws in the puzzle's design matter little. The Harvard freshman of the first novel's title is Russell Bernard, a beautiful and brilliant black student found dead near the Charles River. Lauren suspects members of her freshman seminar on the Russian Revolution, most of whom seem to have had strong feelings of one sort or another about Russell, and begins to investigate with her best friend, another Harvard freshman named Michael Hunt. Their investigation finally reveals the killer and his motives, but first it takes them, and the reader, through a sort of primer on life at Harvard and on their fellow students, incorporating subplots on antiapartheid activism, black/white tensions, pressures on students to achieve academically, drug use and abuse, and sexual behavior. The solution to the murder is anticlimactic, as it reveals that the murder was not peculiar to Harvard or to any university, but could have happened nearly anywhere: Russell was murdered by a drug dealer who was afraid Russell would go to the police with information on the dealer's connection to an earlier death.

In *Radcliffe,* setting, plot, and theme are more tightly connected, as the murderer of one student turns out to be another student "desperately eager to believe that she was better than other people" (p. 173):

Freshman year at Harvard is famous for bringing out everyone's insecurities. At orientation the freshmen are told over and over again that they are the most brilliant, most talented, most important eighteen-year-olds in America, and naturally they wonder if they really deserve to be a part of such a group. (p. 175)

One student has invented a relationship with a famous poet to convince others she deserved to be part of this group, her roommate has discovered the lie, and the lying student has killed the roommate to prevent the lie's being made public. After Lauren identifies the murderer and her motive she thinks about Harvard's particular influence:

Everyone who wants to impress people ends up telling either little lies or big lies. And here at Harvard everyone wants to impress everyone, because we deceive ourselves into believing that everyone else is so impressive. And besides, there are so many people here with famous connections. . . . Who could guess that Helena's connection to Augustine Wedgwood was a complete fabrication? . . . The point is that for Helena the possibility of possessing a certain talent was not enough. Especially at Harvard it wasn't enough. She had to be a great liar and deceiver, and even at Harvard we were all simple enough to be deceived. Maybe because we're so preoccupied with how impressive everyone is and how impressive we want everyone to think we are. (p. 188)

Silver's two novels view the academy from a student's perspective, using the likable although fairly ordinary Lauren Adler as a mediator between the reader and the institution. Lauren is, like most students, far less concerned with the meaning and the continuing survival of the academy than she is with where she might fit into that institution; the focus here is on dorm and social life, not on what goes on inside the classroom or on the life of the mind outside the classroom. Fellow students are infinitely more interesting than are the rather shadowy professors, although Silver does a nice job in *Harvard* of showing Lauren's near infatuation with a seemingly unapproachable female professor and the younger woman's dawning recognition that the professor is not only or exclusively a professor, but also a human being with her own conflicts and weaknesses. Silver's books are marketed as adult mysteries, but their content seems geared to a young-adult reader, especially the frequent digressions about current crushes and budding adolescent romances. I felt, and think most adult readers would feel, a certain distance from these novels, and perhaps even some impatience with the characters' deepest concerns; nevertheless, I was fascinated by Silver's deft portrayal of a young feminist coming to grips with the complexities of a privileged life. In most ways, Lauren holds herself apart from Harvard instead of fully identifying herself with it. Her stance is characteristic of the outsider/insider, who has a legal and moral right to be "inside" yet realizes how precarious her status is and maintains an ironic distance from those really on the inside. Silver seems intrigued by people in this position, populating her books with nontraditional Harvard students: gays, blacks, Jews, Asians, foreigners, working- and lower–middle-class men and women. Lauren's nascent feminist consciousness prompts her to reflect on difference, including her own difference from the self-assured, straight white male students and from other outsiders, such as the members of the National Black Students Lobby in *Harvard*.

Like J. S. Borthwick, Silver uses a modified Bildungsroman pattern in her mysteries, tracing Lauren's maturation while following her through the problem-solving process. Unlike Borthwick, though, Silver has her heroine confront social issues in personal ways that enhance her psychological growth. For instance, in *Harvard*, middle-class Jewish Lauren is powerfully attracted to Russell, the black student who gets murdered, and has to deal with her own attitudes toward race and with others' varying degrees of racism. Her investigation into Russell's death forces Lauren to try to see things from his point of view, until finally that imagined perspective becomes part of her own consciousness. A scene in which Lauren attends a showing of *Gone with the Wind* with a white

Southerner emphasizes the expansion of consciousness that is a side effect of the investigation. Lauren has read *Gone with the Wind* several times and seen the movie on perhaps a dozen different occasions, always identifying with Scarlett O'Hara; she fully expects to enjoy her usual fantasies about the movie this time (p. 177), and at first she does:

And then Mammy appeared, and Lauren began to feel a bit less rhapsodic. Lauren had always known that *Gone with the Wind* was considered offensive to blacks on account of its caricatures of the slaves. Lauren preferred to overlook this criticism of her favorite film, and to tell the truth, she herself had always enjoyed the antics of Mammy and Prissy and Pork. Now, however, after her intensive preoccupation with Russell Bernard, she was not entirely at ease. She could not keep from imagining what it would be like to see this film with Russell instead of with Scott. (pp. 177–78)

Although Lauren doesn't try to imagine exactly how Russell would feel about *Gone with the Wind,* imagining seeing the film *with* him shifts her attitude toward the film itself, making it impossible for her to go on overlooking criticism of *Gone with the Wind* by making its offensiveness concrete instead of abstract.

As one might expect in books whose main characters are young adults living away from home for the first time, both *Harvard* and *Radcliffe* also have a great deal to say about emerging sexuality. Lauren's sidekick Michael is gay, a choice that enables Silver to incorporate discussions of sexual identity unobtrusively into her novels. During her first investigation, Lauren learns that Russell had a sexual relationship with Scott, the white Southerner, and begins to believe Scott killed Russell, especially when she hears Scott speak hostilely of gays. Silver's rendering of Scott's homophobia draws particular attention to the role terror plays in heterosexism. Having been raised in an aggressively heterosexual, masculinist culture, Scott feels true "phobia" about his own homosexual desires, especially when he considers how others would react to his relationship with Russell: "He feared . . . the unimaginably powerful contempt and disgust which his secret would surely inspire in his father, his family, and the entire Richmond society to which he belonged. It was impossible that he, the self-proclaimed product of his own upbringing, should not feel for himself some of that same disgust and hatred" (p. 186). In *Radcliffe,* Lauren deals with her own lesbian desires without the intrusion of homophobia, a difference attributable primarily to the sociology of gender and to the nonsexual ways Lauren finds to act out these desires, such as sleeping fully clothed with her friend Emily and, with Emily, dressing as a man and asking women to dance with her.

The sexual element of Lauren's and Emily's friendship remains partially buried; however, Silver scatters a number of scenes through *Radcliffe* that suggest sexual tension between the two young women. In the first, Emily remarks that she thinks the final scene of *Othello* "is just incredibly sexy" and Lauren agrees. The two act out that last scene, with Emily as Othello and Lauren as Desdemona, then are visited by a relentlessly heterosexual, ultrafeminine woman against whom both Lauren and Emily define themselves, and end up lying together on Emily's bed, drifting off to sleep as they listen to harp music and to the sounds of heterosexual sex from an adjoining room. The intensity of Lauren's and Emily's friendship, their deep connectedness, deserves to be acknowledged as a lesbian feeling. Adrienne Rich uses the term "lesbian continuum" to describe a "range . . . of woman-identified experience; not simply the fact that a woman has had or consciously desired genital sexual experience with another woman."[3] And I would place Emily's and Lauren's relationship on this lesbian continuum, especially because that continuum makes it possible to acknowledge the erotic, but not genital, elements of their relationship. Silver's acceptance of the naturalness of the erotic in relationships between women calls into question her portrayal of Lauren's entirely heterosexual physical sexuality and her choice of a man as a "best friend." Despite her evident interest in the lesbian continuum and her acceptance of male homosexuality, Silver includes no self-identified lesbian in her novels nor does she allow Lauren to imagine a sexual relation with a woman, enacting in her fiction the "compulsory heterosexuality" Rich analyzes without addressing why Lauren, like most women, redirects her search for love toward men.[4] Silver's apparent acceptance of compulsory heterosexuality for her heroine is certainly not unusual, but is puzzling, given the author's manifest interest in relationships between women, homosexuality, and female sexuality—a cluster of concerns that never wholly interconnect in her novels.

Silver does explore the related question of androgyny in *Radcliffe*, with her treatment of this theme offering a possible explanation of her evasion of lesbian existence. Emily and Lauren dress as men for an April Fools' Dance, renaming themselves Laurence and Emil. Lauren stares "with endless fascination at the young gentleman in the mirror" who looks "profoundly alluring. He was, of course, herself" (p. 150). Then Emily joins Lauren at the mirror:

Emily leaned an elbow on Lauren's shoulder in parody of gentlemanly camaraderie, the same leaning pose that Lauren had often seen her bring to bear upon imaginary lampposts; it was one of the fundamental tricks in any mime's repertoire. Now, however, following upon the utter transformation of their appearances, Emily's pose made Lauren feel as if she herself were some sort of imaginary lamppost, as if, in substance, Lauren Adler no longer existed. (p. 150)

The cross-dressing is Emily's idea and later at the dance itself Emily has no trouble finding a woman to dance with, but Lauren is rejected by her choice, who sees that she is really a woman and says "Get lost: what do you think I am, some kind of dyke?" (p. 154). The only time Lauren dances is when Emily asks her to dance to "Macho Man," the Village People's gay send-up of masculine stereotypes. They look like two men dancing together, so people stare, making Lauren feel "tremendously embarrassed and at the same time jubilantly titillated" (p. 155). After a few minutes, many same-sex couples begin to dance: "Out of the closet and into the Fishbowl, thought Lauren, reflecting that this was just the sort of thing that *would* happen when Emily was around" (p. 155). This sequence of events suggests that Lauren is deeply and unalterably feminine and, more specifically, heterosexual, with her sense of self, her identity, enmeshed with her heterosexual femininity: she feels she "no longer exist[s]" when dressed as a man and cannot fool others into thinking her male. Her fleeing from the woman who asks if Lauren thinks she is "some kind of dyke" points to Lauren's fear of being mistaken for a "dyke" herself. *Male* homosexuality is more acceptable to Lauren than female, as indicated by her mixed embarrassment and titillation at being thought half of a male gay couple. Emily, on the other hand, is the initiator of every action in this cross-dressing adventure and is comfortable enough in male garb to fool others, suggesting that Emily's sense of self is not dependent on others' acknowledgment of her heterosexuality or conventional femininity. Emily is freer than Lauren, in other words, to explore androgyny. I think this episode also implies that Emily would be interested in experiencing other parts of the lesbian continuum, whereas Lauren holds herself back: Lauren is more thoroughly indoctrinated into compulsory heterosexuality than is Emily. However, in the two Silver novels, Lauren begins romances with quite a few men—including one to whom her friend Michael is also attracted—but none reaches the level of intensity of her relationships with Emily and with Michael, leaving open the possibility of further experimentation and exploration in future novels.

Gender issues are central in Carolyn Heilbrun's scholarly work, especially in *Reinventing Womanhood* and *Toward a Recognition of Androgyny,* and in the mystery novels she writes as Amanda Cross. There are now eight novels in Cross's Kate Fansler series; read in the order of their publication, the books reveal an increasing interest in feminist questions concomitant with a diminishing commitment to the murder mystery as traditionally defined. With *The Question of Max* (1976), Cross begins to ask what effects male-dominated society has on women, offering a series of tentative answers symbolized by the male criminals and the female victims of the novels. *Max* says that some men will destroy women to maintain their privileges, while also showing the ways in which exclusively male institutions warp men. *Death in a Tenured Position* (1981) looks at three possible female responses to exclusion—imitation of men, entire avoidance of men and of patriarchal institutions, and bonding with other women while continuing to participate in patriarchal institutions in hopes of changing those institutions from within—with the mystery's solution effectively demonstrating the danger of the first of those responses: Janet Mandelbaum dies because she finally despairs of acceptance as an

honorary man. The victim in *Sweet Death, Kind Death* (1984) i
a brilliant, independent woman whose theories about the aging
process challenge received wisdom about women's lives and
threaten the infinitely more conservative work of the man who
kills her (aided by his wife, a male-identified woman). The solution to the mystery in *No Word from Winifred* (1986) underscores
male fear of women bonding together: Winifred "disappeared"
because her lover threatened to kill his wife and children unless
Winifred removed herself from his world. The man's motive for
such desperate measures is his discovery that Winifred and his
wife have become close friends. These last four novels probe women's writing, female friendship, and female development, with
these themes most deeply explored in *Winifred,* which is also the
least conventional of Cross's Fansler novels, despite its many ref-
erences to Kate as Holmes and to her niece Leighton as Watson.

In the first of Cross's novels, *In the Last Analysis* (1964), the
mystery presented is an end in itself, with the solution of the
puzzle presumed to be the dominant interest of the reader, as it
is of the detective and, apparently, of the author. Kate Fansler is
the only fully developed character in this novel, with even Kate's
lover Reed Amhearst and her friend Emanuel Bauer, the falsely
accused psychiatrist for whom she undertakes the investigation,
remaining flat characters who serve limited functions and who
excite little interest beyond their relationships to Kate and to the
puzzle. Like most of Cross's novels, *In the Last Analysis* owes much
to Dorothy Sayers; however, this first Cross novel is indebted
more to the Sayers of the rule-enamored Detection Club and of
the early Wimsey novels than it is to the Sayers of *Gaudy Night,*
with Kate seeming nearly a female incarnation of Wimsey:
wealthy, upper-class, somewhat eccentric, well-read, a believer in
honor and in justice. Even the reasons Kate articulates for agreeing to find the real murderer in order to remove suspicion from
Emanuel echo Sayers's abiding faith in the intrinsic value of
work;[5] Kate tells Reed that Emanuel "and others like him, love
their work; and if you want my recipe for integrity, find the man
who loves his work and loves the cause he serves by doing it" (*Last,*
p. 63). The murderer turns out to be someone who does not
love his work, indeed who *has* no work of his own, but who has
stolen the work of another for financial gain. There are Harriet

Vane-ish undertones in Kate's refusal to marry Reed Amhearst and in her commitment to the intellectual life, but for the most part Cross seems to model Kate on Wimsey and on other male detectives. One critic believes this "imitation of male models" to be "undoubtedly conscious and deliberate," using Heilbrun's comments on masculine role models in *Reinventing Womanhood* to illuminate Cross's depiction of Kate.[6]

Jeanne Addison Roberts notes Heilbrun's urging women to adopt male models "for autonomy and achievement,"[7] but ignores the context of this recommendation, even though the context tells us more about Heilbrun/Cross and, by extension, about Kate Fansler than does the recommendation itself. The passage in question appears toward the end of the opening chapter of *Reinventing Womanhood*, titled "Personal and Prefatory," after Heilbrun has discussed her own early life, women who reject the conventional female role, and women who "made it" in the male world but "failed to bring other women with [them]" (pp. 30–31):

There will appear to be, at the heart of my book, an inherent contradiction. On the one hand I deplore the fact that women of achievement, outside the brief periods of high feminism, have become honorary men, have consented to be token women rather than women bonded with other women and supporting them. On the other hand, I find that those women who *did* have the courage, self-confidence, and autonomy to make their way in the male-dominated world did so by identifying themselves with male ideals and role models. I want to tell women that the male role model for autonomy and achievement is, indeed, the one they still must follow. But if women's best hope of accomplishment is to follow male examples, am I not encouraging the very thing I deplore? (p. 31)

Heilbrun goes on to sketch out a possible reconciliation of this contradiction, suggesting that women need to find ways to achieve in the male-dominated world "in larger numbers" than they have in the past and "without being co-opted as honorary members of a male club" (p. 32). Roberts does Heilbrun a disservice by reducing this complex acknowledgment of contradiction to a simplistic command that women accept role models in order to achieve. From my perspective, the real problems with the passage quoted above are its unexamined assumptions about the nature of achievement and the goals of feminism. Heilbrun here accepts both the masculinist definition of achievement as outward success in the existing hierarchy and the popularized, liberal reduction of feminism to merely a process of adding women in to preexisting institutions; she also assumes that female bonding has to do mostly with women helping other women in this process of adding in. These problematic assumptions make their way into the Fansler series, where one sees Kate, at least in the early books, as quite happy playing the traditional professorial role without worrying much about that role's limitations or about the patriarchal structure of the university. Kate, like her creator, seems to think herself a born feminist,[8] but operates on such a limited definition of feminism that there is no need for her to question just what it is she thinks she is doing as a professor or just how compatible the academy is with feminist values and attitudes.

Judging from *Reinventing Womanhood*, Heilbrun might argue that generational differences among feminists account for differing definitions of feminism and that Kate is true to her generation's experience. Heilbrun created Kate as a near contemporary, a happily early–middle-aged woman in *In the Last Analysis* who evidently believes youth to be overvalued. In the first pages of *Reinventing Womanhood*, Heilbrun speaks of her own pleasure at being fifty, and later describes convening a group of tenured women faculty at Columbia in 1971, all of whom were in their forties or more (pp. 46–47). She found in this small group commonalities that she believes made possible their achievement in a largely male profession: most did not identify with other women or with feminine roles, many were immigrants or members of some other nonmajority group, and most were either only children or from all-girl families (pp. 48–49). Applying Margaret Hennig's work on executive women to these academic women,[9] Heilbrun argues that many may have been chosen by their fathers as substitute sons and therefore probably saw their fathers as role models (pp. 50–52). The autobiographical information Heilbrun includes in this chapter shows clearly why she saw her father as "the only possible role model" (p. 52), as she details what she considers her mother's failure in life and her father's determination to escape the limitations, as he saw them, of his Russian

Jewish origins. The biography Heilbrun invents for Kate—rebellious daughter of a wealthy family, Kate becomes an independent female academic, single and childless—seen in the light of her autobiographical sketch looks like a reinvention of herself without the complications or pain.

Above all else, Heilbrun seems to perceive autonomy as the most desirable possibility for women, criticizing those women writers who do not create autonomous female characters. For Heilbrun, autonomy equates with the notion of a self; she phrases her criticism as "women writers (and women politicians, academics, psychoanalysts) have been unable to imagine for other women, fictional or real, the self they have in fact achieved" (p. 72). Given this set of ideas—that autonomy is essential to a woman's ability to achieve a self and that women writers have seldom created autonomous female characters—Cross's insistence on Kate's autonomy in the abstract but Kate's actual *lack* of autonomy in the concrete becomes especially intriguing. Roberts explains moments that she calls "lapses" in Kate's autonomy—Kate's reliance on men for help, Reed's actually solving two of the mysteries, Kate's peculiar reasons for agreeing to marry Reed in *Poetic Justice*—as results of genre restrictions: "In these cases . . . the conventions of masculine mystery stories and of romance have obscured Heilbrun's goal of depicting the autonomous woman" (p. 10). Roberts goes on to point out the classic detective's total autonomy on a "divine" model and to say that "When the detective is a woman, the risk is even greater that romance and dependency will undercut her already precarious authority" (p. 11). Here, Roberts double-damns Cross: on the one hand, Cross fails in her portrayal of Kate by *accepting* genre conventions, while on the other, she fails by *violating* genre conventions, with the overriding assumption being that male detectives are worthier models than are heroines of romance. In fact, however, Cross begins by accepting genre conventions, modeling Kate on earlier male detectives such as Peter Wimsey, but her commitment to classic detective fiction diminishes with each successive book as her interest grows in the implications of a feminist critique for the crime novel. At no point does Cross borrow without revising conventions of the romance. In the first two novels in the Fansler series,

Kate's gender makes little difference, but beginning with *Poetic Justice* (1970), the various social and cultural issues with which all the Cross novels are concerned[10] begin to be subsumed by the meaning of gender and of gender roles, which becomes the true, albeit covert, object of investigation. By *No Word from Winifred,* overt and covert investigations have merged completely: to answer "What happened to Winifred?" in the sense of "Where is Winifred?" Kate must answer "What happened to Winifred?" in the sense of "What were and are the conditions of Winifred's life?"

As Cross has Kate investigate murders and the conditions of her own life, the author modifies and develops the detective's character so that Kate moves from the position of "honorary man" to more androgynous, autonomous being to woman who identifies *as* a woman and *with* other women. As her conception of the female detective's role shifts, Cross's perception of the victim's and killer's roles also undergo major revisions. In *In the Last Analysis,* the fact that the (second) victim is female matters as little as the fact that Kate is female; what counts in this novel is not gender but work, especially intellectual work, and honor, as traditionally defined for men. By the second Kate Fansler novel, *The James Joyce Murder* (1967), Cross has begun to ask, "Who kills what kind of woman and why?" but the answers in *The James Joyce Murder* and in *The Theban Mysteries* (1971) are tinged with antifeminism, as the female victims are perceived as monsters who somehow deserved killing. Beginning with *The Question of Max,* though, all of the Cross novels offer more complicated and compelling answers to these questions, with the answers forming part of a carefully constructed critique of society from a feminist position.

I would argue that as Heilbrun's understanding of and commitment to feminism have deepened over the years, she has found it progressively less satisfying, perhaps even less possible, simply to add Kate Fansler in to the pantheon of all-knowing male detectives and therefore has begun to experiment with possibilities, revising the genre she began simply by accepting. The initial experiment—putting a woman in a traditionally male position—does little to challenge genre boundaries, as Kate plays a male role in a patriarchally constructed text: the detective functions as an exemplar of inviolate reason, restoring order to a chaotic world while resisting personal entanglements. The murderer in *In the Last Analysis* is completely ruthless, eminently undeserving of Kate's or the reader's sympathy; consequently, the reader is encouraged to accept Kate's trust in the legal system to provide justice in this case. Kate reads the clues in a way identical to the methods of any male detective; similarly, we are asked to read this novel as (actual or honorary) men. Apart from the victim—a young woman "sacrificed to male ambition," as Roberts succinctly puts it (p. 5)—and Kate, the only significant female character is Nicola, Emanuel's wife, an intelligent but uninteresting because unindividualized woman.

Kate steps out of the male detective's role in *The James Joyce Murder*, but not into a reinvented female detective's role; instead, Kate's vacated place is taken by two men, Reed Amhearst and Emmet Crawford, who solve the mystery without Kate, who merely forms part of the audience for their revelation of truth. The victim is a thoroughly obnoxious woman whom Kate describes as having "all the endearing characteristics of a bobcat" (p. 84); the lawyer Reed and Kate hire calls Mary Bradford's death "an act of sanitation" (p. 75), and Kate does not disagree, having earlier described Mary as "like a threat of war, or a strong suspicion that one is pregnant; it is literally impossible to think of anything else. . . . The woman does fascinate. She is so absolutely certain of her own rightness and so absolutely, offensively wrong on every possible count" (p. 39). The killer gets all the characters' sympathy in this novel, with even District Attorney Reed describing his arrest and probable imprisonment as "ghastly" and hoping he can plead insanity (p. 167). Reed claims that "the only real sinner . . . was the woman he killed" (p. 168). Mary's sin—apart from being voluble and gossipy—was using blackmail to seduce the young man who killed her. William, the killer, is apparently driven to murder by academic pressures and by losing his prized sexual chastity. Kate's strange passivity in *The James Joyce Murder*, her relegation to a supporting role, is explicable only if one thinks of this novel as a thematic and developmental bridge between *In the Last Analysis* and *Poetic Justice* (1970). Having initially placed Kate in the male role, Cross now seems to be having doubts about her detective: if a woman's stepping into male shoes is not entirely satisfying, what else is possible? *The James Joyce Murder* works through what I see as a failure of imagination by placing Kate in a very nearly conventional female role, but Cross is obviously dissatisfied with this possibility as well, reconsidering the whole genre of detective fiction in her next novel, *Poetic Justice*, which also reworks the theme of academic pressures central to the puzzle's solution in *The James Joyce Murder*. Here one finds that William made blackmail possible by hiding a Joyce manuscript in hopes that discovering it would assure his success in the publish-or-perish world of academe.

Two themes in *The James Joyce Murder* illuminate Cross's decision to place Kate on the sidelines. The first is the theme of what work and sexuality might mean for women, explored through examining the lives of five female characters: Kate, who proclaims herself a woman committed to a profession, taking lovers but not marrying; Mary Bradford, sexually and intellectually frustrated, a destroyer of men, who tries to repress her sexual desires beneath prudish disapproval of others' "orgies"; Lina Chisana, a young PhD who sees her virginity as a "burden" and worries obsessively about William's refusal to engage in premarital sex (pp. 116–17); Grace Knole, a retired, distinguished professor and self-described "childless old maid" (p. 159); and Molly, Mary Bradford's "replacement," who appears to have been born to bear children and to fill happily and attractively the traditional feminine role. Of all these women, only Kate has both meaningful work and sex; however, she is unsure she has love: Kate seems to think it nearly impossible for a woman to have both work and love or, most especially, work and a husband and children. Taking care of her nephew Leo for the summer and staying in the same house as Reed (and assorted others) is a way of trying out marriage and motherhood while continuing with her professional life (she's editing some of Joyce's letters). The second theme is that of authorship/authority and focuses on Padraic Mulligan, author of pseudonymous best-selling novels whose success has enabled him to force his publisher into issuing his mediocre criticism, the sheer volume of which has got him promoted to full professor. Mulligan, who ought to be ashamed of his poor scholarly work, is actually deeply ashamed of his sex-and-violence books, so much so that he booby-traps Kate's car in hopes of preventing her discovery of his secret. Heilbrun, who did not reveal her authorship of the Amanda Cross novels until after she was granted tenure at Columbia, seems to be poking gentle fun at herself and less-gentle fun at academe through Mulligan, but beneath the humor lies a quite serious attempt to work out her own goals in creating Kate Fansler.

The words that Heilbrun/Cross has Grace Knole, a woman one is given ample reason to respect, speak to Kate may apply also to the author's motives in writing *The James Joyce Murder.* Kate says that Reed has asked her to marry him but she is fearful that the proposal shows only that "we all fall apart in the middle years" (p. 159). Grace responds with:

Jung has a theory about human life I'm rather taken with.... He thought that about age forty ... a human being needed to remake his life because, in a certain sense, he had become a different person.... He believed in discovering who it was you were trying to become. (pp. 159–60)

Kate tries to object, but Grace interrupts, telling her "We'll argue another time. I wonder if you didn't get involved in this peculiar summer because you knew this kind of stasis was somehow needed, the protection of the womb before birth" (p. 160). The peculiarities of *The James Joyce Murder* may be aspects of an intentional stasis in Cross's characterization of Kate, with the novel itself—in which Kate does little, leaving the investigating and numerous decisions to men—a temporary womb before the birth of a remade Kate in *Poetic Justice.* In the latter novel, Kate decides to marry Reed, reconsiders her commitment to her university, begins to revise her view of her profession, and, most significantly, becomes a different sort of detective than she was in *In the Last Analysis.* Her rebirth is not complete, though, as it is once again Reed who solves the mystery.

Both victim and murderer in *Poetic Justice* are men—the sole male victim in the Fansler series—but the murder is accidental and Reed, instead of marching the confessed killer off to the police, decides to keep the truth quiet by placing a leading account of the accident in the case file. The crime here is depicted as an accidental mercy killing: hoping to make an insane professor take a leave by causing him to become ill, another professor substitutes aspirin for the victim's own medicine, but the plan misfires when the man turns out to be fatally allergic to aspirin. The academy is more centrally significant to *Poetic Justice* than it is to either *In the Last Analysis*, where Cross treats departmental politics with wit and humor, or to *The James Joyce Murder*, where only the publish-or-perish syndrome plays a role. *Poetic Justice*'s murder takes place at an English Department party and is one part of a larger plot focusing on the very idea of the university, as faculty members fight over the fate of an adult education division; further, this plot is interwoven with consideration of campus radicalism and student opposition to the Vietnam War.

The center of interest in *Poetic Justice* is not the puzzle of who killed Professor Cudlipp—the murder doesn't occur until more than halfway into the novel and then the investigation is directed by Reed—but Kate's increasing involvement with University College, the threatened adult education division, and the personal growth that involvement both spurs and reflects. Near the beginning of *Poetic Justice*, Kate reflects on the events of the previous spring, when student protesters took over buildings and were clubbed by police called in by the administration, and thinks of her own feelings, which include "a love for the University which was irrational as it was unrewarded" (p. 18). Trying to figure out "what it was she loved," Kate decides it is "inexplicable. The love one shares with a city is often a secret love, Camus had said; the love for a university was apparently no less so" (p. 18). At the end of the novel, Kate again tries to understand her sense of "what did one call it, affection, love, devotion?" and again fails: "Yet how explain this love? Suffice it perhaps to say that here was an institution for which she would willingly work; the University was not, for her, simply a place wherein to pursue a career. I recognize the claim, she thought, even if I cannot recognize what it is that makes the claim" (p. 163). Kate's attitude toward the university parallels many of the less radical 1960s and 1970s protesters' attitude toward the US: they loved their country, but hated what it was doing in Vietnam and, much as Kate scorns the university's administration and its board of governors, objected to its leaders. Judging from the rest of *Poetic Justice*, what Kate loves is the ideals the university embodies, the promise of what it could be: a place where all are welcome to share in the life of the mind. This loyalty to the university's ideals is what prompts Kate to work for the survival of University College against those whose elitism threatens to destroy both University College and the university itself.

The best characters in *Poetic Justice* are dedicated to their work but able to achieve balance in their lives, unlike the most radical students, who are portrayed as seeking only to destroy, and the most reactionary professors, who seek only stasis. Cross illustrates the value of balance through both negative and positive, serious and humorous examples. The funniest is the bizarre, bordering on the psychedelic, dissertation defense in which Cross sends up every academic hobbyhorseist in just a few hilarious pages. Professor Peter Packer Pollinger, whose very name is a joke and who at first appears to be unable to dismount his personal hobbyhorse, turn-of-the-century Irish author William Sharp and his female alter ego Fiona Macleod, is the most amusing and most attractive example of balance, demonstrating shrewd insight into his colleagues and wide-ranging knowledge. Most importantly, Pollinger represents the virtues of androgyny, a combination of male and female, through his intense interest in Sharp/Macleod. This emphasis on balance explains Cross's decision to marry Kate and Reed in *Poetic Justice,* as their union symbolizes Kate's achievement of balance between love and work. She tells one colleague that she has believed "that marriage for a woman spoils the two things that make life glorious: learning and friendship. Somehow, that no longer seems so unquestionably true" (p. 31) and later tells another that although Forster's comment that "the abandonment of personality can be a prelude to love" is true "for most women," for Kate "it hasn't been" (p. 75). In other words, Kate realizes that, with Reed, she can be both half of a "partnership" (p. 50) and her own self, that she can have love and work, learning, friendship, and marriage. Cudlipp's murder fits into the theme of balance: having become mentally unbalanced because of his inability to balance love and work, his past at University College and his present prestigious position at the university, he dies trapped in an elevator that he has sabotaged as part of a fanatical plot to discredit radical students. Cross's choice of murderer is thematically significant as well, as he is a professor Kate has in the past "worshipped" (p. 53) and then avoided knowing well for fear of discovering he was unworthy of her adoration. The campus unrest and Cudlipp's death afford Kate the chance to find a more realistic view of this man, to see him as her equal, neither god nor fallen god.

The rebirth hinted at the end of *The James Joyce Murder* is effected in *Poetic Justice*, with Kate markedly more mature and self-accepting in the later novel than in the earlier. The last page of *Poetic Justice* mentions the marriage of Kate and Reed in the fashion of Victorian novels, but in no way is this marriage the apotheosis of Kate's being: it is simply the beginning of a new stage in her life, an *addition* to that life and not a substitution for all that has made her life "glorious." Marriage, like academe, is an institution worth preserving despite its defects, *Poetic Justice* implies, and Kate's decision to marry Reed complements her decision to help University College, with both choices indicative of Kate's growth.

However, three novels later, we find that Kate has lost much of her faith in institutions, and even in the very university she is said to "love" in *Poetic Justice*. *Death in a Tenured Position*'s first chapter finds Kate deciding, while at a committee meeting, "that this decade would be marked for her by the sitting around tables, . . . in the company of many men, and a few women, whose assignment was to grapple with the problems of academia in the seventies" and imagining "her tombstone with 'The Token Woman' engraved in the marble" (p. 4). Shortly thereafter, she is annoyed with herself for responding to "something attractive" in a lesbian who "hated male institutions" (p. 15) and who has implied that Kate is a patriarchal woman, one who is "worse than a man" because "she conspires with men against other women" (p. 12). As she investigates Janet Mandelbaum's life and death, though, Kate realizes that her belief in the power of *any* institution to "operate fairly" is largely a matter of will (p. 70). Kate's casual affair with an old lover in *Death in a Tenured Position* indicates some loss of faith in marriage as well, or perhaps more accurately, since Kate has never professed deep faith in marriage as an institution, an attempt to reassert her autonomy. She describes her interest in institutions as "a morbid fascination," saying "they are so implacable. I can't take my eyes off them, as though they were a grotesque sideshow. And I want terribly to be present at the moment they begin to shake and change" (p. 58).

Cross's four novels following *Poetic Justice* consider academe anew, but in two—*The Theban Mysteries* and *The Question of Max*—the academy considered is not a university but a private secondary school, one a girls' and the other a boys' preparatory school. The girls' school, the Theban School, is portrayed as nurturing, responsive to its students' needs, and dedicated to the ideal that learning should be a mutual experience; its headmistress, Miss Tyringham, is an antisnobbish, flexible woman and the Theban reflects her values. Cross here blends ideas of earlier feminists, most notably Mary Wollstonecraft and Virginia Woolf, by creating an institution that offers girls useful preparation for adulthood and that upholds an androgynous ideal, giving its female students so good an education that all of its graduates "found college an anticlimax of almost unmanageable proportions" (p. 19) and imbuing them "with a tomboy, bluestocking attitude" they never really lose (p. 18). In contrast, the boys' school described in *The Question of Max* reflects the values of the Watergate conspirators and of the so-called "me decade" of the 1970s, with the headmaster of St. Anthony's covering up several boys' cheating because "he'd rather not rock the boat" (p. 96). Even before Kate knows about the cheating and the cover-up, Cross has her contemplate her "distaste for St. Anthony's": "St. Anthony's was as different from the Theban . . . as the jet set from Back Bay" (p. 69). Kate asks herself whether the difference is that between boys' and girls' schools generally, but quickly decides not (p. 70). Regardless of Kate's dismissing this possible explanation, *The Question of Max* suggests that it is indeed the difference between all-male institutions and those to which women are welcomed, or at least admitted. When read together, *Death in a Tenured Position*, set at Harvard, and *Sweet Death, Kind Death*, set at a women's college in western Massachusetts, operate as revisions of *The Question of Max* and *The Theban Mysteries*, respectively, with *Sweet Death, Kind Death* also acting as a corrective to the implication of *Death in a Tenured Position* that it is prestigious, originally all-male colleges that most oppress women. The women's college in *Sweet Death*,

Kind Death as an institution embodies Janet Mandelbaum's attitudes, hostile to feminism and to feminists, run by a president who is doing her best to be an honorary man.

Although *The Theban Mysteries* has some important feminist elements, such as the marvelous portrait of the bright, interested and interesting young women students in Kate's *Antigone* seminar and the way in which Reed and Kate share equally in the detection, this novel is very troubling when read from a feminist perspective. The victim—not of murder, as it develops, but of a heart attack brought on by overhearing her children speak the truth— is a mercenary, useless woman, neurotic and hysterical, whom Kate decides is "absolutely better off dead" (p. 168). Roberts suggests that Cross kills off Esther Jablon as a symbolic cleansing through destruction of a woman "who represent[s] for her [an] antiquated mode of female behavior" (p. 5), linking this purging with passages in *Reinventing Womanhood* that argue for the need for new female models (p. 5) and pointing out the "streak of anti-feminine rage" one finds in *The Theban Mysteries,* "a rage directed specifically and unforgivingly at the failures of the older generation of women" (p. 6). The dead woman gets no sympathy from Kate or from Cross, beyond a rather cursory tacit acknowledgment that Esther was shaped by a woman-hating society (pp. 134–35). *The Question of Max* reads almost like an apology for *The Theban Mysteries,* as the novel focuses steadily on male-dominated institutions that shut out women and by so doing create environments in which hatred for women and disrespect for others in general flourish. The victim in this novel is Geraldine Marston, a young graduate student planning a dissertation on a woman writer, while her killer is Max Reston, an elitist and antifeminist who believes all who disagree with him are fools (p. 202). Victim, murderer, and motive in *The Question of Max* echo those of *In the Last Analysis,* as a man kills a woman in order to appropriate work that is not rightfully his and to maintain his professional status, a situation and motive Cross uses again in *Sweet Death, Kind Death.*

Max's killing of Gerry makes literal the theme of the erasure of women in society that forms one part of the argument for women's equality in *The Question of Max.* Cross relates this murder to the cheating/cover-up at St. Anthony's, to the Watergate conspiracy, and to the elitism and sexism of universities like Oxford, seeing all as representative of what happens when masculine self-worship goes unchecked by female influence. Kate's friend Phyllis makes the Oxford parallel to the murder clear when she begins a letter to Kate with "This is from me, Phyllis, your friend that was. I am no more because there is no place for women at Oxford, be they neither students nor dons" (p. 84). Max makes the error of believing himself to be a superior being by virtue of his sex and class, an error that twice causes him to be thwarted in his plans by women who do not accept cultural valuations of gender. On the first occasion, Cecily Hutchins, a famous writer who had planned for Max to be her literary executor, sees what Max is really like when he remarks that "at least she had been a good wife," telling him, "I don't think you understand anything" (p. 206), and soon thereafter deciding he is "wrong for [her], as literary executor and certainly as biographer" (p. 207). On the second, Kate figures out that Max has forged letters from another woman writer when she thinks about the letters' frequent repetition of a hope that the writer's child will be a boy, and realizes that the woman "would never have wished for a boy that way or harped so on it" (p. 204). As she tells Max, "Women are not all as self-hating as you assume them to be" (p. 204). Max has admitted that "a feminist, a free-thinker, a socialist, and a pacifist" is "everything I loathe. Nor am I reconstructed when it comes to women. I like them to be ladies, wives, and mothers, or at worst, eccentric and appealing old maids. If they write novels, as Cecily did, they should do it when their womanly duties have been fulfilled" (p. 181). Max's hatred of women enables him to kill Gerry Marston without remorse and to try to kill Kate—who, in a sorry retreat from a new independence and centrality as detective, is rescued at the last moment by Reed—making Max the most villainous of Cross's murderers, yet Cross shows compassion even for him and for those like him. Reed says that Max is "certainly mad" (p. 214), a remark that implies the possibility of Max's receiving treatment instead of imprisonment for his crimes. With this ending, Cross acknowledges that men, as much as women, are products of their society and that even the most antifeminist of men should be reeducated, not destroyed or cut out of a new order. She also suggests that misogyny is a sort of disease or disability, amenable to treatment.

There is no woman in *The Question of Max* who fully accepts the patriarchal order, but such a woman features prominently in *Death in a Tenured Position,* whose solution illustrates the dangers of accepting that order's definition of women. This novel fictionally works out the theoretical heart of *Reinventing Womanhood*[11] by setting a woman who consents to be a token woman (an honorary man) against both women who refuse to participate in the male world and women who achieve in the male world while bonding with and supporting other women. Janet Mandelbaum, the woman who is happy to be chosen as Harvard's token, believes in the face of overwhelming evidence to the contrary that her sex is irrelevant, that women's studies is "nonsense" (p. 102), and that if women were "good enough" (like her) they would be employed at prestigious universities (p. 103). Her ex-husband says that "all her life Janet has ignored other women, even despised them" (p. 53), a comment that confirms Kate's own observation that Janet has "turned her back upon the whole idea of women; [at her former university] she had operated within her department, had been accepted, at least to her satisfaction, as one of the boys" (p. 49). Janet's failure to see the truth—that Harvard hired her *because* of her sex, that she can never really be "one of the boys," that gender matters—gives Kate the major clue to the puzzle of Janet's death. Janet committed suicide when a male colleague forced the truth upon her at a department meeting, telling her directly that Harvard has been "saddled" with her and that the least she can do in return is teach the women's studies courses he also thinks are "nonsense" (pp. 138–39). Janet takes cyanide, but it is clear that she has been metaphorically poisoned long before her actual death and that the male world in which she had achieved by imitating men murdered her. There is no need for a man like Max to kill a woman like Janet, since she cooperates in the obliteration of (female) self, proving the truth of Kate's earlier observation that "there is no place for women" at Harvard (p. 12).

The separatism of the group of radical lesbians Kate meets is certainly not self-destroying, as Janet's attitudes are, but is portrayed in *Death in a Tenured Position* as undesirable. Significantly, though, the reader is given no real reasons to reject separatism beyond Kate's (and the author's) obvious disapproval, a disapproval smacking of heterosexism. Through the positively portrayed female characters—Sylvia, Kate, Penny, and Lizzie—Cross comes down strongly on the side of liberal feminism, advocating success in the male world and bonding with other women. Sylvia articulates the novel's theme in a conversation with Kate: "Whether or not women change their lot will depend on their future friendships, what Virginia Woolf called something more varied and lasting because less personal" (p. 108).

The theme of female friendship is at the heart of *No Word from Winifred* as well, wherein Cross describes two intense friendships between women, one in the past and one the friendship that leads to Winifred's disappearance. Winifred's friendship with her lover's wife, Biddy, fits the definition of friendship borrowed from Woolf as "less personal." Biddy tells Kate that "neither of us had many friends—women friends, I mean—who were interested in ideas and in reconsidering the set boundaries of women's lives. . . . I was lonely for women friends—most of the women in my community were fine, but they weren't like me; they didn't explore in the same way, they accepted what they were told, and they chatted too much about domestic details" (p. 161). Kate completely sympathizes, saying that "the scarcity of women friends—I mean friends who were out in the world and had more to talk of than recipes and toilet training and what to wear—well, that's known only by the few of us who had only male friends in those days" (p. 161). When were "those days"? The novel is set in late 1983 and early 1984, and Biddy is described as being around forty, placing "those days" in the 1960s or early 1970s and making Biddy something of an anachronism. The disquisition on female friendship may be Cross's way of responding to feminist criticisms of Kate's lack of involvement with other women, but it is a less than satisfying explanation. Kate has no intense friendships with other women, and no friendships of any kind that last beyond a single novel in the series. She seems able to connect most closely with dead or otherwise-absent women—Cecily Hutchins in *The Question of Max*, Patrice Umphelby in *Sweet Death, Kind Death*, and Winifred Ashby in *No Word from Winifred*—and to make that connection through reading the woman's work. In that sense, Cross keeps Kate true to the image of the classical detective, diluting the feminist themes of her novels. Although the novels after *The Theban Mysteries* insist that Kate is no honorary man, Cross persists in placing her in an isolated, masculine position.

It may seem from the space and time given Cross's Kate Fansler series that Cross is the only woman writer with a female academic detective, but that is not the case; I do think, though, that Cross is the most influential of the writers in this genre and Kate Fansler the most complex and interesting detective. While it is true that the Cross novels present some problems to feminist readers, it ought to be said that they present far fewer problems than do any other mysteries in their category.[12] For example, Susan Kenney's Roz Howard books—*Garden of Malice* (1983) and *Graves in Academe* (1985)—both conclude with the female detective nearly murdered by the villain she has failed to detect, saved at the last moment by a man. *Graves in Academe,* a totally conventional mystery of the puzzle variety based in part on false literary clues, begins with Roz denying that she is a feminist—exactly the sort of statement Kate Fansler deplores in *Death in a Tenured Position*—except of the "existential" kind. As she later reveals, "her main activity over the years [has] consisted of seeing to it that no one ever got away with discriminating against her or anyone else in her vicinity and her profession on the basis of sex, or anything else, for that matter" (p. 45). *Graves in Academe* includes some interesting and realistic descriptions of classroom discussion and in that limited sense is more of the academic world than are the Cross novels,[13] but Howard seems little interested in considering the larger academic and gender issues the Cross novels contemplate. Most importantly, even the weakest Cross novels are far better plotted than either of Kenney's books, which have such convoluted plots that they often seem downright silly. *Graves in Academe,* for instance, asks one to involve oneself in a series of murders and incidents of vandalism based on a course syllabus, evidently committed by someone dressed in a Ninja outfit who is trying to frame both an art professor and a student. Kenney drops so many clues that the criminal's identity is no mystery well before the supposedly shocking revelation scene in which—I am not joking—a mask is literally ripped from a man's face, "revealing the strong chin, the tight-lipped mouth, the stern, darkly enraged visage of—" and here either Kenney or her editor leaves 4½ lines of white space before giving the killer's name (p. 260), which anyone with a bit more intelligence than the characters in the novel evince would know already.

I like the fact that Cross never resorts to the slash-and-trash style of teen movies from which Kenney seems to be borrowing, with bodies piling up but attracting little police attention and a heroine not smart enough to protect herself even after she has been attacked once. Poor Roz Howard just seems to happen upon murder and mayhem, a problem for series detectives that Cross neatly solves by having Kate stumble across only one murder in the series—in *The James Joyce Murder*—usually being asked by others who respect her intelligence or who have heard of her detecting hobby to help solve problems. Kate is seldom arrogant about her abilities—on the contrary, she is often plagued by self-doubt—but the reader never doubts those abilities, even when Kate is proved wrong. When Kate reaches (temporarily) a false conclusion in *The Question of Max,* her error contributes to the overarching theme of people's prejudices and assumptions blinding them to reality, showing Kate as human, less than perfect. Similarly, when she mistakenly concludes that Winifred is dead and confronts the supposed murderer, her momentary arrogance is shaken by the man's confession of his real actions, which are in some ways more shocking and revealing than would be his confirmation of Kate's suspicions. In both instances Kate learns something about herself from her error, whereas Roz Howard seems unfazed by her inability to solve the mystery in *Graves in Academe.* Perhaps some of the distaste I feel for this novel comes from my own prejudices: it is hard for me to accept that a former English professor would go on a killing spree because he thinks his desire to be a college president may be thwarted by a student and by some disgruntled faculty members. The piling of murder upon murder at little Canterbury College in *Graves in Academe* ultimately makes it impossible to continue suspending disbelief. Problems of believability are, of course, lessened when the detective is not an academic or other amateur but a police officer whose job it is to investigate murders, the category of detective I consider in the next chapter.

4

New Procedures for Police?

The police procedural, a relatively new subgenre of the crime novel, appeared first in the United States in the 1950s, with Ed McBain's books generally considered among the earliest examples of the genre (Symons, p. 194). Among the most rigidly formulaic of crime novels, police procedurals usually take the point of view of the police detective, offering exhaustive details of police routine in investigating a crime or, occasionally, several crimes, and frequently bringing in some details of police officers' private lives in order to establish characters' personal interest in the crimes they solve (Symons, pp. 193–94). Police procedurals assume interest in police routine on the part of the reader, who presumably is not a police officer; consequently, the crime being investigated often gets short shrift, giving way to details of the investigation itself: the crime is the excuse for the investigation, in other words, with larger questions of justice, human psychology, and social order taking a secondary or even tertiary position to the minutiae of daily life in a police station. The many limitations of the subgenre relate to its valuing verisimilitude over psychological realism; as Julian Symons points out in his brief treatment of police procedurals in *Bloody Murder,* surface realism is essential in these novels, making them especially suitable to television adaptation (pp. 193–94). The recent popularity of police shows—even those that do not rely on weekly doses of big car chases, gun battles, or sensationalized crimes, such as *Hill Street Blues* and *Cagney and Lacey*—suggest widespread public interest in police routine. It is the nature of this interest, taken for granted by writers of police procedurals and by creators of television cop shows alike, which requires some examination.

The police are one of the official mechanisms of authority, and perhaps the most visible representatives of social order. Like other institutionalized forms of power and control, most significantly the armed forces, police departments are hierarchically organized, subject to a complex system of regulations, and authorized to enforce yet another complex system of laws. They are also largely a closed system whose workings are mostly mysterious to those outside that system. This mysteriousness may explain some of the fascination of police procedurals for lay people, as may the police officer's paradoxical position as both figure of power and authority to the general public and powerless hired hand in service to higher authority within the hierarchy of his/her department. Police departments remain largely male, mirroring in this nearly exclusive masculinity other male homosocial institutions; even the organization representing police officers in many cities is called the Fraternal Order of Police, a name that calls attention to the self-conception of police officers as members of a brotherhood, which by definition excludes women.

What happens when women try to join this brotherhood? Does the brotherhood cast them out, change its own shape to accommodate sisters, or force the women to become brothers, male police officers in female bodies? Before turning to novels featuring women police detectives, I want to examine a nonfictional account that implies some answers to these questions, Marie Cirile's 1975 *Detective Marie Cirile: Memoirs of a Police Officer*. Although I realize Cirile probably had little control over her book's jacket, the front cover inadvertently symbolizes the schizophrenic elements of Cirile's account of her seventeen years as a New York City police officer: above the bold white letters of the title is a photograph of a female hand—carefully manicured, with long red nails and numerous gold bracelets hanging from the wrist—with the index finger on the trigger of a gun. Awkwardly written and often difficult to follow, Cirile's memoir nonetheless fascinates in its mixture of clear-eyed criticism of a police department's inequitable treatment of male and female officers and the author's confused response to that treatment. Cirile does not seem to have sorted out her experiences in a way that would help her to make sense of them, and, on one level, the book suffers from that failure; on another level, though, it is precisely this failure that is so intriguing, as it reveals the conflicts inherent in the term "woman police officer," if one imbues each part of that term with conventional associations.

Cirile joined the police force on the urging of her sister Lee, taking the civil service examination in 1956 as a sort of lark, "just for laughs," but also because her husband, a cop, said, "Don't be ridiculous, what the hell makes you think you could ever pass the same kind of test I took?" (p. 8). Her background—daughter of highly traditional Italian immigrants, herself married young to an equally traditional man—superficially seems an unlikely one for a policewoman. Cirile says that she was "brought up to believe that any man knows better than any woman," in a household that assumed all women's destiny to be marriage and motherhood and that prepared each of its girls "to serve this God creature she will marry: to obey, to cook, to clean, to bear children (boys, preferably), and to keep her mouth shut, because after all everyone knows women were put on earth to suffer" (p. 3). What Cirile does not acknowledge, however, is that in some ways her background was ideal preparation for filling the role of policewoman as it was constituted in 1956 and, indeed, for most of her seventeen years on the police force. Female recruits "were tolerated, or worse yet treated as pets" by their male classmates in training school (p. 13). When they graduated from the Police Academy, they were assigned to the Policewomen's Bureau, where their duties were public extensions of conventionally feminine, private, familial caretaking tasks: guarding female prisoners in detention cells and hospitals, guarding female witnesses, operating lost children's shelters at beaches and parks, and the like (pp. 18–21). An ambitious director of the Policewomen's Bureau developed specialized arresting squads, eventually responsible for six hundred to eight hundred arrests annually, but her apparently threatening success resulted in the police department's disbanding the bureau and sending the policewomen to precincts, where "they went back to being matrons, making coffee, sewing on buttons, smiling and looking pleasant, and if they had a progressive-thinking desk officer, answering the switchboard or entering summonses" (p. 23). These women were excluded from the brotherhood of police officers, but remained part of the police family, playing the role of daughter to their paternal bosses, never sister to the police officer brothers.

Cirile realized that she was being discriminated against on the basis of sex—denied challenging assignments, paid less than her male counterparts, told by one representative captain "I do not want women in my squad. . . . I don't want my men distracted" (p. 93), transferred out of units as soon as she showed expertise and initiative—but her response to this discrimination was self-defeating. Instead of making common cause with other women, Cirile internalized the male officers' hatred of women and determined to make herself different, a strategy often employed by members of oppressed groups.[1] This memoir is studded with criticisms of other women, the most revealing of which is Cirile's description of what she calls the "Miss Goody Two-Shoes" syndrome: "a condition sown and cultivated by the men, and adopted and nourished by certain of the women who basically disliked work and found this attitude"—of being too feminine to "compete on the same level as a man"—"the perfect answer to their goofing off" (p. 44). Cirile recognizes the genesis of these women's attitude, but doesn't seem to realize that her own attitude is equally self-defeating and equally male-engendered; her determination to make detective by "killing them [the brass] with quality work" (p. 117) implies a fundamental failure to see the true dimensions of the problem of discrimination. To borrow Carolyn Heilbrun's terms, Cirile became a sort of "honorary man," measuring herself in terms of her difference from other women. Instead of feeling outrage at the terms in which a commanding officer compliments her, for example—a misogynist who wants no women on his squad, he tells her she is not like "all the rest" of the women and says he would like her to stay "when the other girls get transferred out" (p. 105)—Cirile finds herself "sniffly" because she has just "been handed an accolade that always seemed just beyond [her] reach" (p. 105). This response is emblematic both of Cirile's adoption of male definitions and values, a fusion of the values of her traditional background and of the patriarchal police department, and of her vision of herself as an exception. A poignant reminder of Cirile's basic traditionalism comes in a section of the book that deals sketchily with her private life: her husband beat her but Cirile always blamed herself, finally finding the courage to leave him only after years of abuse. Although she tells of freeing herself from one oppressor, Cirile never fully realizes the extent of her oppression outside of her own home, remaining convinced to the end of the memoir that her hard work and loyalty to her brother officers somehow matters. *Detective Marie Cirile* suggests that the brotherhood of police officers will try to cast out female intruders, who may in response try to become male officers in female bodies; the brotherhood itself does not change just because some women batter at its doors or even get a foot inside them.

The resistance police departments display toward women who would enter—and by entering, begin to redefine—them finds a parallel in the police procedural's resistance to female, and particularly feminist, revision. Lillian O'Donnell's Norah Mulcahaney is Marie Cirile's fictional counterpart; like Cirile, Norah is an NYPD officer during the department's expansion of policewomen's duties and must work against her male peers' and superiors' efforts to "protect" her by keeping her on desk duty or assigning her other conventionally feminine tasks. Also like Cirile, Norah is married to a police officer, in an interesting fusion of personal and work lives. O'Donnell kills off Norah's idealized husband Joe, having him die in a grisly on-duty disaster early in the series, a maneuver that allows O'Donnell to involve Norah with other men without compromising the character's staidly conventional morality. Norah is conventional in other ways as well, most significantly in her dedication to the ideal of law and order as defined by the patriarchal authority for which she works and in the organization of her private life. Jane Pennell, in "The Female Detective: Pre- and Post-Women's Lib," describes Norah as "more feminine than feminist," saying that the character's "job is in a field that has been liberated from male domination, but her private life continues to be lived, in a sense, under male dominance" (p. 92). Contrary to Pennell's confident assertion, police work has not been "liberated from male domination" and never

will be as long as power remains patriarchally defined and constructed. Norah's private life mirrors her professional life, as *both*
are lived under male domination.

Lillian O'Donnell's plots and themes tend to be deeply anti-
feminist, despite superficial nods in the direction of feminism
through Norah's musings on the ingrained antifemale attitudes
of her colleagues and superiors. *No Business Being a Cop* (1979)
documents the slight raising of Norah's consciousness through
her investigation of a series of murders of policewomen that
seems to be the work of a man obsessed with ridding the NYPD
of women officers. Early in this novel, the reader is told that
Norah subscribes to the "killing-them-with-quality-work" theory
of advancement:

Policewomen had not gained the acceptance in the department that the
public thought they had. Discrimination was still practiced subtly and
sometimes not so subtly. However, Norah felt she personally had established her own credentials as a detective and, particularly since she'd
made sergeant, rarely ran into resistance anymore. When she did, as
now, she ignored it; she'd learned it was the best way. (p. 18)

Ignoring "resistance" does not make it go away, as Norah eventually realizes when her captain tries to prevent her speaking to
a policewoman's group:

She had never been an active women's libber. Norah believed in individual
initiative; she thought that those women who had ability and diligence
would achieve whatever they were after. Banding together was good, but
it was not a substitute for each woman's putting out her best. . . . She had
thought that the women in the police department had definitely come a
long way. Was she wrong? [The captain's] attitude clearly indicated that
the rights the women thought they'd won on merit and hard work, standing beside the men, working the same hours, taking the same risks, were
rights not earned but conferred. Conferred by the grace and favor of the
men. She had never been so angry in her whole life. (p. 101)

This anger is as far as O'Donnell takes Norah, dropping the issue
of women's rights directly after this passage and then creating
a chaste near-romance between Norah and the captain whose

paternalism has prompted her (brief) awakening from her dream of achieving equality through "ability and diligence."

Norah's romantic interest in this captain implies acquiescence to his self-described "old-fashioned" views; at the end of the novel O'Donnell suggests Norah's discomfort by having her suspect the captain of the murders, but never links this discomfort directly to her early stirrings of feminist awakening. Furthermore, the importance of this discomfort and suspicion is undercut by the result of the investigation that the novel details. Norah and the other officers on the case operate on the assumption that the killer is an enraged male police officer, killing women he believes have taken men's jobs. Norah solves the crime not through ordinary police procedures, but by accident after her own life is endangered. The killer is a male dupe of his sister, a "sweet, innocent, fragile" woman (p. 252) who has been involved in thefts and drug deals; his motive was not "hatred for . . . policewomen in general" but "love—for his sister" (p. 254). The solution to the crimes suggests that women are the source of crime, manipulating men to do their evil bidding, which places *No Business Being a Cop* squarely in the tradition of detective stories that concentrate on the treachery of women[2] and that endorse stereotypical views of women. Norah's mild, budding feminism is completely trampled by the messages given by the rest of the novel.

O'Donnell's *Ladykiller* (1984) is more viciously antifeminist than *No Business Being a Cop,* and is the reason I stopped reading the Norah Mulcahaney series. Again, there are hints of a superficial feminism, as Norah meets sexist resistance while trying to work cooperatively with a male detective from a suburban police force on a series of murders; again the victims are female; again Norah begins a romantic relationship with a male detective from whom she initially meets professional resistance; again Norah solves the crime accidentally, only after reaching a false conclusion and endangering her own life (do police officers really work as decoys in murder cases as often as police novels suggest?); and again the killer turns out to be a male dupe of a manipulative woman. O'Donnell's villain in *Ladykiller* is a combination of the treacherous, sexually predatory woman and the denying mother, a fusion of two stereotypes illustrative of male fears about women. Magda

Petrus is described as unfeeling and sexy, using her body to en-snare her son and her husband in a web of crime. Norah at first sees her as one stereotype—"a woman torn between her roles of mother and wife"—but shifts to another after looking at "her dirty house, her expensive clothes, her scent, her fake jewelry," now viewing her as "self-indulgent, a woman who would stop at nothing to get what she wanted" (p. 216). The reader learns that Magda has encouraged her son's stealing even from churches and poor boxes, and then pushed her husband to kill the son and four young women, all because she loves money and herself. If, as I suggested in the first chapter, some feminist crime novels ask "who kills women and why?" O'Donnell's police procedurals an-swer that women have men kill other women for money and for male attention. Implicitly, then, these novels offer justification for male domination and patriarchal structure by presenting a view of women as dangerous and lawless, with Norah and several other policewomen perceived as exceptions to the general rule. Looked at from this angle, Norah's dedication to patriarchal order is what saves her from sinking into the uncivilized muck inhabited by women who rebel against that order.

O'Donnell's series does not push back the boundaries of the police procedural subgenre, apart from placing a woman in the detective role; because Norah Mulcahaney is essentially a patriar-chal woman, though, this alteration makes little difference. In contrast, Barbara Paul's *The Renewable Virgin* (1985) subtly ques-tions some of the basic assumptions underlying police procedur-als. Although not part of a series, Paul's novel deserves dis-cussion here because of its deliberate engagement with the issues O'Donnell brushes against but then evades in *No Business Being a Cop* and *Ladykiller*. The O'Donnell novels endorse a traditional conception of the police officer, who is seen as owing his or her loyalty to other officers (his/her "brothers") and to official order (his/her "father") while ignoring the limitations of police proce-dure except to note women's ability to escape justice. In both novels, the male pawn is arrested but the stories close with the implication that the female mastermind will remain untouched by the law. *The Renewable Virgin*, on the other hand, draws attention both to the limitations of police procedure and to problems inherent in traditional conceptions of loyalty and police solidarity through Paul's method of narration. At the same time, one gets a detailed, sympathetic, and entirely believable treatment of a woman's consciousness-raising and a highlighting of the identification between police detective and victim implied by many police procedurals. Paul accomplishes all this by abandoning the usual limited-consciousness or omniscient narrative of crime novels, substituting instead three personal narrators, all women, each of whom speaks in a distinctive voice, contributes to the solution of the crime, and offers a unique perspective on the investigation and on the other narrators.

Because of the method of narration, *The Renewable Virgin* is not technically a police procedural: the reader does not follow the investigation entirely from the police detective's point of view, as only one of the three narrators is a police officer. In addition to New York City cop Marian Larch's narrative, the story is told by an actress, Kelly Ingram, and by the victim's mother, history professor Fiona Benedict. Furthermore, police procedure alone does not lead to the solution to the mystery; instead, Kelly Ingram and Marian Larch each reaches the solution independently, with the former following a combination of intelligence and intuition and the latter following police routine, orders from her captain, and material provided by Fiona Benedict. This novel also violates linear progress, as the three narratives are complexly recursive, with multiple clusters of interest beyond the solution of the murder. Paul here fuses elements of at least three different varieties of crime novel: the police procedural (through Marian); the celebrity amateur detective novel, like Anne Morice's Tessa Crichton, Antonia Fraser's Jemima Shore, and Paul's own Geraldine Ferrar series (through Kelly), and the academic mystery (through Fiona).

Each of the women narrators works within a particular, patriarchally ordered, closed system, with academe, television, and police departments all portrayed as rigidly hierarchical structures in which all power is concentrated in the hands of a few men. Marian and Fiona seem to know the boundaries of the worlds they inhabit before the novel opens, with Fiona adopting as her own the rules of the system in which she lives and works, convinced (how familiar this sounds!) that fair play by these rules will result in the same rewards for her as those enjoyed by her male colleagues, and Marian more clear-sighted about the limitations of her position as a woman police officer. Kelly, in contrast, seems to have given no thought to the entertainment industry's treatment of women as salable commodities, in spite of her recognition that her role in a television series makes little use of her talents while making much use of her body and of her acknowledgment that her agent "sometimes calls himself a flesh-peddler. I think he dislikes women. His speech is just full of little put-downs" (p. 44).

Fiona Benedict instantly, intensely, dislikes Kelly, seeing both Marian and Kelly as "part of an alien, violent world that I did not care to be on a first-name basis with" (p. 25), but reserving her scorn for the actress. After seeing an episode of the television show in which Kelly stars, Fiona's dislike hardens:

Her role was that of an adjective describing the noun hero. She was the sexually available but eternally fresh female, experienced innocence personified, the kind of woman whose virginity is renewable upon demand. We were supposed to think that if Lefever could have a woman like that gazing upon him adoringly, then he must be one hell of a man. The same little-boy notion of manhood that has always kept women prone in a male society. I wasn't too surprised to find the Ingram woman helping perpetuate the notion. (p. 56)

Fiona's analysis of the role Kelly plays is certainly accurate, but she mistakes the woman for the role. Then, too, the intensity of her hostility is remarkable, stemming as it does from her unwillingness to see similarities between herself and Kelly. Fiona has spent fourteen years researching and writing a biography of one of the English commanders in the Crimean War—subscribing, in effect, to a masculinist, "big men and big wars" conception of history and thereby helping to perpetuate yet another "notion of manhood that has always kept women prone in a male society." This refusal to recognize the truth is characteristic of Fiona, who tells everyone that her husband deserted her and her son when in fact he committed suicide and later pretends that her son died of an allergic reaction to medicine when he actually was murdered. Fiona has managed to convince herself that she is first a historian and only second or third a woman, denying connections with other women while allying herself with male historians, yet it is always women who aid her: Kelly bails her out of jail and gets her a lawyer when Fiona attempts to shoot a popular historian who has written a book on "her" subject; Marian offers comfort and support after her son's death; and, most tellingly, the wife of a male colleague, not the colleague himself, leaves home to help Fiona when she is in trouble. In *The Renewable Virgin*, Fiona represents a model of womanhood just as problematic as, and perhaps even more soul destroying than, "the sexually available but eternally fresh female" popular on television programs.

Marian's point of view is more tolerant than Fiona's, and more nurturant of growth. She sees Kelly's role in the television series and her plans to judge the Miss America contest as having a "prostitutional aspect" (p. 98), but believes that Kelly is capable of growth and change. She understands why Fiona Benedict would have no respect for Kelly, while not subscribing to Fiona's view: "Kelly wasn't an educated woman. . . , but that didn't mean she was stupid. . . . Kelly never kidded herself about what she was doing for a living or tried to pretend it was anything more than it was" (p. 67). In a distinctly unfeminist move, Fiona merely dismisses the Kelly Ingrams of the world, whereas Marian, in true feminist fashion, sees value in *all* women and helps Kelly to raise her consciousness. *The Renewable Virgin* is more a novel of feminist awakening than it is a police procedural. Marian solves one murder through documents provided by Fiona, following police routine; police procedure is inadequate in the investigation of a second, related murder, but Kelly's newly raised consciousness results in her discovering and trapping that killer. No more is heard about the killers after they are carted off, presumably for arrest, trial, and punishment, and in this limited way the novel follows a conventional pattern, with order restored and the violators of order shut out from society. In a most unconventional conclusion, however, Paul ends *The Renewable Virgin* with hints of a lesbian relationship beginning between Kelly and Marian, with Kelly offering to "cheer [Marian] up" by staying at her house and Marian agreeing, saying Kelly is "always welcome—any time at all" (pp. 184–85). Kelly has the last words, addressed directly to the reader and evocative of the "happily ever after" formulation of romances and fairy tales: "Aren't those nice words to end a story with?" This lighthearted, upbeat ending neatly encapsulates the overall tone of *The Renewable Virgin*, which plays exuberantly with the conventions of crime novels, taking very little seriously. Even the idea of murder, secondary as it is to the feminist consciousness raising, has little impact in this text. Although there are three murder victims in *The Renewable Virgin*, these victims seem curiously unreal to the other characters and are certainly insubstantial for the reader, who never sees the victims alive and learns little about their lives beyond the manner of their leaving them.

Susan Dunlap's three Jill Smith books, *As a Favor* (1984), *Not Exactly a Brahmin* (1985), and *Too Close to the Edge* (1987) conform more closely to the conventions of the police procedural than does Paul's novel, but also test the boundaries of that genre in ways that neither Paul's book—because of its extreme divergence from the police procedural's methods—nor O'Donnell's Norah Mulcahaney series—because of its basic conservatism—does.[3] Dunlap circumvents having to address some of the problems a woman police officer might be expected to experience by making Jill a member of a fairly unconventional police department and by giving her a black commanding officer in the first novel, thereby creating a reasonable expectation that gender bias would play a lesser role in Jill's life than it might in the life of a woman police officer in a traditional department under the command of someone insensitive to prejudice. On the first page of the first Jill Smith novel, Dunlap has Jill draw attention to Berkeley's difference from other police departments as she recalls the 1969 struggle for People's Park: "But during those angry days, the Berkeley Police calmed animosities on both sides. To residents they were a different breed, better educated, more liberal, as much 'Berkeley' as police. . . . Now, years later, it was still a police force I was pleased to be a part of" (pp. 1–2). This insistence on the Berkeley police's difference neatly sidesteps some issues of power and of motivation, suggesting that one need not be a law-and-order type to wish to be part of that department while presenting the average Berkeley cop as a benign, peace-loving character. The reader is told that Jill joined the police force nearly by chance, after moving to Berkeley so that her husband could go to graduate school and "after searching for the right job to fill the interval before we moved on to some ivy-covered little college where he would begin his climb up the academic ladder" (*Brahmin,* p. 112). Jill decided to take "the Patrol Officer's test hoping for a job to support us during that time. Our stay in Berkeley was to be temporary, a necessary period until Nat graduated and our real life began" (*Favor,* p. 12). The Berkeley police department quickly turned into Jill's real life, however, as she learned that she both enjoyed and was good at her work, with her personal growth eventually leading to a divorce from Nat. Although ambitious and interested in moving up the police department ladder, Jill is not especially dedicated to abstract ideals or to the law itself, nor does she view other officers as her brothers. Dunlap presents Jill as a new type of officer in a department in which computerization and masters degrees in management fuse with the "Berkeley-ism" of the officers to create an especially progressive police force. *Too Close to the Edge* is the only one of the Jill Smith books to suggest that even Berkeley police have the reputation of misusing power, with Jill worrying that an advocate for the handicapped will parlay an encounter with the police into news. However, the novel suggests that this is an image problem with no basis in fact, for readers observe the entire episode and see that Jill does not harass anyone; indeed she tries to help the woman when her wheelchair's battery gives out.

As a Favor emphasizes the limitations of even such a benign, progressive police department by tracing Jill's investigation of a disappearance and possible homicide that turns out to be chimerical, with Jill's investigation actually causing a murder that might not otherwise have happened. While investigating a nonexistent crime, Jill moves ever closer to discovering an actual crime, with the fear of discovery finally driving a woman to kill her partner. This novel is largely about the ways in which one's assumptions limit one's perceptions, with a minor character articulating the theme while giving an important clue to the mystery early in the book when he tells Jill that actors rely on makeup to give an audience a certain impression: "Once you give them the major clues, they fill in around them . . . [makeup is] a lie with internal consistency" (pp. 87–88). Even after this discussion, Jill persists in misreading the clues, filling in around false assumptions. When she goes to a woman's apartment and finds it in disarray, with signs of a struggle and blood stains, she believes the woman is missing, possibly dead. She also believes this same woman, a welfare department social worker, was helping her clients cheat and skimming some money from their checks in a kickback scheme. Putting both beliefs together, Jill assumes the woman was murdered by one of her clients. Once she becomes aware of the way in which she has been supporting false assumptions with other false assumptions, Jill is able to sort out the truth—the white welfare worker was actually running a much more complex scam, eventually "disappearing" in plain view by disguising herself as a black welfare client—but her awareness comes too late to prevent the murder.

By focusing on Jill's persistent misreadings, Dunlap prompts the reader to consider the notion of authority. It is Jill who tells her own story, and the reader sees her being wrong more often than right, with the chances very good that the reader is reading the novel with the same faulty assumptions Jill brings to her reading of the case. Once Jill discards these erroneous assumptions, it becomes clear that all along there were other, more accurate deductions she might have made from the same clues, but that her preconceived ideas led her consistently to choose the false over the true. The efficacy of police procedure in general is called into question in *As a Favor*, as we realize that police routine has provoked a major crime (murder) by failing to deal adequately with a minor one (welfare fraud). Similar misreadings—but misreadings with far less grave consequences—operate in *Not Exactly a Brahmin,* in which the clue to a murderer's identity lies in examining assumptions about race and gender: a figure everyone in the novel assumes all along is a Vietnamese male turns out to be a white woman. Again, the reader is given an important hint early on by a minor character, this time Jill's new commanding officer, who tells her he assumed a woman detective would be "too soft," someone "who got too emotionally involved with the widows, who didn't want to ask the tough questions" (p. 100) and therefore never expected to have to deal with a complaint that a woman officer was "badgering the widow" (p. 101). Granted that playing on assumptions and encouraging misreadings are standard tactics in detective fiction, Dunlap's Jill Smith books probe the implications of such misreadings with more than the ordinary interest; nevertheless, Jill always does figure out the truth in her cases, learning by the end of each novel to read the clues from a different position.

In the first two Jill Smith novels, the murderers are women and the victims men, with money a significant part of the motive. The victims in neither case are especially sympathetic, with the one in *As a Favor* the killer's partner in a criminal scheme and in *Not Exactly a Brahmin* a man who has caused his own death by taking elaborate, vicious revenge on a group of people whom he evidently saw as humiliating him. Whereas the murderer and her motive in the former novel are both simple rather than complex— she is an utterly unlikable person driven entirely by greed—both in the latter novel are complicated and far more interesting. Nina Munson kills Ralph Palmerston to save her ex-husband's computer company. Jill's colleague comments that the murder was "such a masculine kind of crime" (p. 209), involving cutting a car's brake lines, and Jill agrees; but it is also a feminine kind of crime, with Nina acting not only in her own self-interest but in the interest of the ex-husband she still loves and in personal anger against a friend (Palmerston's wife) whom she believes betrayed her. The victim in *Too Close to the Edge* is a woman whom Jill knows rather well and with whom she sympathizes. In some ways, then, this novel stays closer to genre conventions, with the police detective's identification with the victim helping her solve the murder by enabling her to figure out how Liz thought and would have acted on those thoughts. The victim, as a paraplegic, also embodies Jill's deepest fear, giving the detective even more reason to feel a personal investment in solving her murder. *Not Exactly a Brahmin, As a Favor,* and *Too Close to the Edge* end similarly, with the criminal arrested and the police detective presenting a presumably accurate reading of the crime, but these conventional endings are called into question by all that precedes them in the novels, with an uneasy, lingering implication that Jill's final reading of the clues is, like all readings, somehow incomplete.

Despite the interesting features of Dunlap's Jill Smith books and Barbara Paul's *The Renewable Virgin,* the police procedural ultimately seems an unpromising genre for the woman creator of a woman detective. Most women writing in this genre accept its boundaries, with Lillian O'Donnell's Norah Mulcahaney series typical of women's forays into it.[4] The police novel is especially resistant to feminist revisions, with its history—it is a subgenre that is aggressively fathered, but not mothered—and its dependence on a surface realism that in turn is dependent on a masculinist system of power together arming it against female intruders, particularly against serious novelists with feminist questions to raise. I have come across only three novels that might by any stretching of genre definitions be thought of as police procedurals that give more than occasional glimpses of what a thoroughgoing feminist reimagining of the subgenre might entail; two are Katherine V. Forrest's Kate Delafield books, which will be discussed in the sixth chapter, while the other is P. D. James's *A Taste for Death* (1987), the most recent of her ten novels and the one most centrally concerned with the role of the police in a murder investigation. Like all of James's work, and unlike the other novels considered in this chapter, *A Taste for Death* is serious fiction, an elegantly written and profoundly troubling examination of religious, philosophic, and social concerns implicit in the murder that sets the plot in motion.

In *A Taste for Death,* James breaks away from her established pattern in the Adam Dalgliesh series of placing a single police officer in the privileged position in the text. Here, Dalgliesh's perspective is balanced and counterbalanced by the perspectives of two other police officers working on his crime investigation team and by those of many of the people caught up in the investigation, with James moving from one consciousness to another throughout the novel, developing overlapping layers of narrative. In effect, the narrative structure of *A Taste for Death* is a more complex and sophisticated version of Paul's in *The Renewable Virgin.* The British James writes out of a different tradition of the police novel than do the other writers considered here; then, too, because *A Taste for Death* employs a woman police officer as only one of three police foci, the novel does not technically fit the model that this

chapter examines. Nevertheless, I want to look at James's treatment of the woman police detective, Kate Miskin, as Kate's role in
the police investigation and the background James gives her in *A
Taste for Death* both raise and resolve some particularly interesting
issues.

Like Adam Dalgliesh, Kate is not only a police detective;
whereas Dalgliesh is a poet, Kate is a painter, with James's implication in both cases being that police work on the one hand requires the kind of attentiveness and creativity one expects from an
artist, but on the other does not offer an adequate outlet for that
creativity. Dalgliesh's writing and Kate's painting provide expression for the part of the self that police work does not engage.
Again like Dalgliesh, who is an orphan raised by foster parents,
Kate comes from a background of deprivation and pain:

She was illegitimate and had been brought up by her maternal grandmother, who had been nearly sixty when she was born. Her unmarried
mother had died within days of her birth and was known to her only as
a thin, serious face in the front row of a school photograph, a face in
which she could recognize none of her own strong features. Her grandmother had never spoken of her father, and she had assumed that her
mother had never divulged his identity. She was fatherless even in name,
but it had long ceased to worry her if it ever had. (p. 165)

Although Kate professes unsentimental lack of interest in her
own history, believing that "she had little feeling for the past;
all her life had been a striving to struggle free of it" (p. 166),
James portrays her as deeply marked by that past, as evidenced
by Kate's need to repress her own longing for mother, father,
and home.

The murder investigation on which Kate works with Dalgliesh
teaches Kate about herself; when at the end of the investigation
she thanks Dalgliesh for choosing her to be on his "murder
squad" and tells him, "I've learnt a lot" (p. 494), the words are
resonant with meaning: she has learned about investigative tech-
niques, but also and more importantly about her job's meaning to
her, her life, her past, and her self. At one point Kate realizes that
she has begun allowing herself to feel empathy, thinking that

perhaps "I can afford a little involvement, a little pity. But it was strange that it should begin now. What was it, she wondered, about the Berowne case which seemed to be changing even her perception of her job?" (p. 349). Kate does not try to answer her own question, but James makes the answer clear to the reader, as the case involves precisely those issues most salient in Kate's background: class privilege and class antagonism, religious experience, family, mistreatment of children, illegitimacy, money, power, sexuality, aging, the privileging of men over women, and, of course, death.

The background James invents for Kate provides a plausible explanation of what might attract a woman to police work. Raised in public housing—poor, her opportunities limited—Kate chose her job "deliberately, knowing that the job was right for her. But she had never, even from the first, had any illusions about it" (p. 211). She acknowledges ambition and a preference for "order and hierarchy to muddle" (p. 355), saying, "I didn't want an office job. I wanted a career where I could earn well from the start, hope for promotion. I suppose I like pitting myself against men" (p. 355). Kate never thinks of the police force as a substitute family or as a brotherhood to which she might be admitted as an honorary brother, nor does she perceive herself as a crusader for justice or even as much interested in abstractions of any kind:

It was a job where you were sometimes required to work with people you'd rather not work with and show respect for senior officers for whom you felt little or none; where you could find yourself allied to men you despised and against some for whom, more often than you'd bargained for, more often than was comfortable, you felt sympathy, even pity. (p. 211)

Kate's pragmatism and her refusal to romanticize herself or her job protect her from delusions about the role of gender: she knows that it is "hard enough for a woman to climb without getting kicked in the ankles on the way up" but treats sex discrimination as simply one of the "disadvantages" of the job (p. 212). She also knows Dalgliesh chose her for his special squad because of her sex, not despite it, accepting this fact of life in a gendered society calmly but valuing herself enough not to internalize the sexism she finds around her.

Kate's choice of career is in some ways a response to sexism and classism; not only does she enjoy "pitting [herself] against men," but she also finds in police work a power generally denied others of her sex and class. She feels "elation" after interrogating an upper-class doctor—"Every minute of her brief confrontation with that self-satisfied poseur had been deeply pleasurable" (p. 205)—acknowledging to Dalgliesh that she "liked the sense of being in control" (p. 206). The more experienced Dalgliesh responds by saying, "No one joins the police without getting some enjoyment out of exercising power. No one joins the murder squad who hasn't a taste for death. The danger begins when the pleasure becomes an end in itself" (p. 206). There is a refreshing candor in this exchange about power, especially because other women writers generally avoid having their female detectives think about the attractions of power, particularly for the socially powerless. Kate's wielding of power never crosses over into the danger zone Dalgliesh identifies, nor does it ever become cruel, perhaps because she does allow herself to feel empathy.

Kate notices a similarity between Dalgliesh and the murder victim, thinking that "the more she learned of Berowne, the more alike he seemed to Dalgliesh" (p. 358); James points to uncomfortable similarities between Kate and the murderer. In both cases, though, there are crucial differences, with the differences between Kate and the killer most interesting because most directly linked to their distinctive responses to deprivation of love. While the killer feels an aggrieved sense of injustice and lack of connection with others—he hates his mother for not loving him enough, his father for trying to disprove his paternity, and his various stepfathers for their lack of care—one that grows to a conviction that the world owes him recompense, Kate comes to value connectedness and to forgive those who wronged her. The critical difference here is empathy, which Kate learns but which the killer can never feel because he is trapped in egoism.

Kate has tried to deny her empathic quality and to preserve her freedom and privacy at the price of refusing to take care of her elderly, extremely annoying grandmother, but decides that people must matter more than job, freedom, or privacy, a decision that opens her to love. When Kate and her grandmother are taken hostage by the killer, they touch for the first time with love (p. 468), with imminent death removing all reserve and resentment between them and the grandmother finally revealing the circumstances of Kate's birth. Although she has repressed her desire to know about her parents for twenty years, when it seems she might die it suddenly becomes important for Kate to know if her mother wanted her, with her grandmother's admission she was indeed a wanted child giving Kate the inner strength to take measures against their captor (p. 473). Ultimately, Kate survives but her grandmother is killed. The killer taunts Kate, saying, "You're free of her now. Aren't you going to thank me?" (p. 487). The words haunt Kate, as she wonders if she did indeed will her grandmother's death. In establishing the significant differences between Kate and the killer, however, James has prepared the reader to see that Kate is not responsible for her grandmother's murder, as Kate has infinitely larger sympathies than does the killer and motivations that transcend his narrow self-interest: Kate will not destroy others to get what she wants, but the killer will, and that is precisely the distinction between them.

As in every other police novel discussed thus far, *A Taste for Death* concludes the investigation with the arrest of the murderer. However, James disrupts the restoration of order by having Dalgliesh ponder the illusory nature of that order; the case may end, the novel may conclude, but murder never comes to closure:

But with murder there never was a final victim. No one touched by Berowne's death would remain unchanged. . . . There was action and there was consequence. (pp. 494–95)

The "ripple effect" of murder defies neat conclusions, refusing to be contained by whatever artificial ending the police, or the author, attempt to fix on it.

James's portrayal of Kate Miskin in *A Taste for Death* points out some of the directions feminist reconsiderations of the police novel might take. Alone among women authors of police novels,

James tackles the thorniest problems: What kind of woman might be attracted to police work and yet refuse to be merely an honorary man? What are the dynamics of power, gender, and class? What is the role of empathy? What is the relation between a woman police officer and traditional conceptions of law and justice? What are the implications of bringing a murder investigation to closure? *A Taste for Death* transforms the genre from which it springs by defying that genre's restrictions; it is therefore a worthy model for study, and one that might serve as inspiration for even more daring revisionary police novels. Significantly, it is the only one of the seven novels discussed in this chapter to repay rereading with fresh insights.

5

Loners and Hard-Boiled Women

In each of Sara Paretsky's four V. I. Warshawski novels, there is a moment when the detective's name becomes an issue. In the first book of the series, *Indemnity Only* (1982), a corporate vice president asks, "What does the *V* stand for?" to which V. I. replies, "My first name" (p. 17), inaugurating what will become a recurring theme: characters want to know what lies behind the initials in order to call the detective by something more feminine and conventional than those initials, whereas V. I. persists in fighting off such intrusions, insisting on her right to name herself. This struggle over the name of the detective acquires increasing significance with each repetition, eventually coming to stand for larger struggles, most especially women's fight for equality and autonomy and women's ongoing attempts to fashion from man-made language expression capable of reflecting female experience.[1] Within the novels themselves, though, the political reasons for V. I.'s insistence on initials or on the androgynous nickname "Vic," which she allows friends to use, disguise her more psychologically significant desire to hide her real name, which she claims simply to hate but which resonates with disturbing meaning: Victoria Iphigenia. Revealing that name, with all of its mythic symbolism, would be the equivalent of revealing her own deepest anxieties, and so V. I. guards it.

90

Paretsky's use of an enormously freighted name for her detective and then her depiction of that detective's obsessive attitude toward her name find interesting echoes in other women writers' practice. Although neither P. D. James's Cordelia Gray nor Liza Cody's Anna Lee tries to conceal her name behind initials, one feels that each should, as the name tells more about the character than is comfortable to reveal instantly. Whereas Paretsky has V. I. finally examine her name's meaning in *Killing Orders* (1985),[2] the implications of their characters' names are left unstated by James and Cody, yet have a kind of magical significance impossible for the reader to ignore. James's Cordelia Gray, like her Shakespearean namesake in *King Lear* is the motherless daughter of an irresponsible, selfish father who sacrifices her happiness—in this case her desire to attend university—to his own wishes. Unlike her namesake, who is eulogized by her father in terms of silence and obedience (Lear says, as he holds his daughter's dead body, "Her voice was ever soft, / Gentle and low, an excellent thing in woman" 5.3.274–75), James's Cordelia learns to ignore the memory of the way "her own voice had irritated her father" (*Unsuitable,* p. 274) and to speak out loudly in her own interest, with the two books in which she is featured following her movement into independent, adult womanhood. Cody's Anna Lee bears little resemblance to Edgar Allan Poe's Annabel Lee, the lost, dead romantic heroine for whom the speaker of the poem mourns. Poe's Annabel Lee is frozen in an eternal childhood ("*I* was a child and *she* was a child"), her dead body fetishized by the poem's speaker, who insists that death cannot separate him from his beloved:

> *For the moon never beams, without bringing me dreams*
> *Of the beautiful Annabel Lee;*
> *And the stars never rise, but I feel the bright eyes*
> *Of the beautiful Annabel Lee:*
> *And so, all the night tide, I lie down by the side*
> *Of my darling—my darling—my life and my bride,*
> *In her sepulchre there by the sea—*
> *In her tomb by the sounding sea.*

Cody brings Annabel Lee back to life, creating her as a speaking subject, an agent of action, instead of Poe's silent, immobile object of the male gaze. On some level, then, Cody is revising literary history, taking the male writer's heroine and turning her into a female hero, freeing her from childhood, romance, and objectification all at one go.

The names of the other two series detectives I will be discussing in this chapter are less obviously symbolic than V. I. Warshawski, Cordelia Gray, or Anna Lee, but have peculiar significances of their own. Sue Grafton's protagonist/narrator has an androgynous, not clearly ethnic name, Kinsey Millhone, with the name's ambiguity and near unplaceability representative of the character's relative freedom from ties of any kind. Similarly, Sharon McCone, the name Marcia Muller gives her detective, seems almost generic. However, Muller takes pains to have other characters in several of her books inquire into the name's origins, with each questioner admitting surprise that the detective looks American Indian but has a Scotch-Irish name; Sharon's name works as a sort of disguise because it does not match her appearance (or vice versa, of course).

Although investing characters' names with symbolic significance is a fairly common literary device, the distinctive associations of these five detectives' names and the characters' sensitivity about them give the issue of naming especial importance in the novels in which they appear. Other characters in these novels often place themselves in particular relation to the detective by their naming of her. For instance, in the first of Marcia Muller's Sharon McCone novels, *Edwin of the Iron Shoes* (1977), the detective develops an uneasy relationship with a police lieutenant, Greg Marcus, who alternately encourages and patronizes Sharon. By the end of the novel the two are moving toward sexual involvement, but it seems clear to the attentive reader that theirs is a doomed romance, with Marcus's insistence on addressing Sharon by an endearment that she finds offensive—"papoose"—one clear indication of trouble ahead. This nickname suggests that Marcus sees Sharon as a child and as an object identifiable strictly by race. In the second of the McCone books, *Ask the Cards a Question* (1982), the reader finds Marcus wooing Sharon with chocolate—still unable to take her seriously—but agreeing in the end to accept Sharon's terms for their relationship, a relationship that meets its inevitable end in *The Cheshire Cat's Eyes* (1983). All the characters in Liza Cody's novels refer to the detective as "Anna" or "Miss Lee," with the notable exception of her downstairs neighbor, Selwyn Price, who calls her "Leo" or "young Leo." A poet, Selwyn might reasonably be expected to hear echoes of the Poe poem in Anna's name; his refusal to use that name suggests a rejection of the name's symbolic import. Selwyn sees Anna for what she is and avoids diminishing her by naming her as the heroine of romance. The name he chooses to substitute calls attention to his perception of Anna's bravery while also hinting at "masculine" qualities. Indeed, Anna handles all the conventionally masculine domestic chores for Selwyn, from fixing his bicycle to repairing various household appliances, and his naming her "Leo" seems an acknowledgment of her greater self-sufficiency. In the fourth Anna Lee novel, *Head Case* (1985), another poet adopts Selwyn's nickname for Anna for reasons similar to those one can infer about Selwyn.

Sara Paretsky's narrator/protagonist actually tells us how to read those characters who call her anything other than V. I. or Miss Warshawski. She allows her friends to call her "Vic," with only Lotty Herschel, her closest friend, consistently using this form of address throughout the four novels, an indicator of their long-standing friendship and mutual respect. In contrast, police homicide lieutenant Bobby Mallory, V. I.'s dead father's closest friend on the police force consistently refers to the detective as "Vicki," a feminine nickname that reflects Mallory's view that "being a detective is not a job for a girl like you" and his wish that she were "a happy housewife now, instead of playing at detective" (*Indemnity Only*, p. 24). V. I.'s family, from whom she is estranged, shares Mallory's disapproval of her career and life-style, asserting their right to judge her by using the name she hates, Victoria. In nearly exact parallel with Sharon McCone's uneasy relationship with a man who refuses to use her correct name, V. I. becomes involved with a man in *Indemnity Only* who first refers to her as "little lady" (p. 19), later insists he cannot call her "V. I." ("Will you tell me your first name? How the hell can I keep on addressing someone as 'V. I.'?" [p. 40], and, after the detective relents and allows him to call her "Vic," then pressures her to reveal her middle name (p. 41). Ralph's inability to accept V. I.'s choice of name is indicative of his deep discomfort with her untraditional job, a discomfort that surfaces also in his desire to protect her and, more dangerously, in his rejection of her solution to the case, a rejection that gets him shot and endangers several other lives, including V. I.'s. Their relationship finally ends with Ralph's admission that, like V. I.'s ex-husband, he "couldn't believe you knew what you were talking about. I guess deep down I didn't take your detecting seriously. I thought it was a hobby" (p. 208). As with Greg Marcus's insistence on calling Sharon McCone "papoose," Ralph's trouble with V. I.'s name is representative of deeper difficulties that doom their relationship from its beginning.

Male detectives do not have the same difficulties with names as do their female counterparts, certainly a reflection of social conditions and power relations, but the names of male hard-boiled detectives do tend to resonate with cultural significance. Dashiell Hammett's Continental Op never reveals his name, with that namelessness suggestive of his total identification with his job.[3] Hammett's Sam Spade, like Grafton's Kinsey Millhone, has a nearly generic, ethnically and socially indeterminate name, but his surname contains a kind of joke about his job—he will keep digging for clues—along with a more ominous hint of the grave, with ominous hints lurking in Grafton's hero's surname as well: she can be a "millstone," a burden, to those trying to hide something because she is very sharp, able to "hone" clues.[4] Raymond Chandler's Philip Marlowe often is the romantic, chivalric figure his name suggests, with his various inquiries into the extremities of human psychology updating his namesake's consideration of the forces that propel Faust into a bargain with the devil. Apart from the importance of names, women writers' female private eyes share various more or less salient characteristics with their hard-boiled male forebears. Of minor significance, but nonetheless noteworthy, is the peculiar concern with "exhaustive details of . . . bathing, dressing and interest in food," which Barbara Lawrence in "Female Detectives: The Feminist—Anti-Feminist Debate," remarks upon, saying that "for some obscure reason, all fictional male private eyes have those traits" (p. 45). In all five series under consideration here, one gets complete catalogs of clothing and food, with Paretsky's V. I. Warshawski, for example, reporting extensively on the style, color, material, and sometimes even the manufacturer (she is fond of Magli shoes) of her clothes, detailing a number of meals in each book, and often commenting on her need for a shower or describing long soaks in her tub. V. I. also drinks a lot, as do Sharon McCone and Kinsey Millhone, talks tough (ditto all but Cordelia Gray), and carries a gun (as do the others, except Anna Lee), all characteristics also of the male private eyes.[5]

Then, too, all the women detectives are urban dwellers, like Hammett's and Chandler's detectives, and their narratives display the kind of extensive knowledge of particular cities—Warshawski's Chicago, McCone's San Francisco, Lee's London—including street names, minor landmarks, and the like, that one finds in Chandler's descriptions of Los Angeles, for instance. In his insightful examination of the genre, "The Hard-Boiled Detective Novel," George Grella notes that the hard-boiled detective is always depicted as utterly exhausted at the end of the novels (p. 110), a pattern repeated in all of the twenty-two novels of the five women's series.[6] Even the characteristically bare style of Hammett's novels, "in which everything superficial in the way of description has been removed" (Symons, p. 125), thereby conveying "a sense of physical and temporal immediacy" (O'Brien, p. 71), finds an echo in Sue Grafton's style in the Kinsey Millhone novels. Here, for instance, is the opening paragraph of *"C" is for Corpse* (1986):

I met Bobby Callahan on Monday of that week. By Thursday, he was dead. He was convinced someone was trying to kill him and it turned out to be true, but none of us figured it out in time to save him. I've never worked for a dead man before and I hope I won't have to do it again. This report is for him, for whatever it's worth.

This style, like Hammett's, is admirably suited to developing a sense of "the sheer gratuitousness of life," in which "events just happen" (O'Brien, p. 71).

The American women creators of female private eyes seem keenly aware of the masculine tradition of the hard-boiled detective, originating in pulp magazine stories between the wars (Symons, p. 123) and carried on in cheap paperbacks with lurid covers into the early 1950s (O'Brien, pp. 4–6). In *"B" is for Burglar* (1985), for instance, Sue Grafton has an elderly woman make jokes about Mickey Spillane, saying she wants to help Kinsey with an investigation, perhaps even be her partner, but first has to prepare for the job: "I'm going to start reading Mickey Spillane just to get in shape. I don't know a lot of rude words, you know" (p. 103). Spillane's novels are extreme examples of the hard-boiled school, perverting the tradition through Mike Hammer's "solipsistic belief in himself, his unerring rightness, his intensely lonely virtue," which "all become a vivid argument for a totalitarian moral policeman whose code, no matter how vicious, must be forced upon every man" (Grella, p. 117). In Grafton's novel, Spillane's books are amusingly reduced to dictionaries of "rude words," deflating the "moral policeman's" self-righteous bombast. Sara Paretsky's third V. I. Warshawski novel, *Killing Orders*, contains a similar moment, when the detective mocks both herself and the hard-boiled tradition when she longs for a bodyguard and then mentally corrects herself: "Of course, a hard-boiled detective is never scared. So what I was feeling couldn't be fear. Perhaps nervous excitement at the treats in store for me" (p. 215). This novel also gives an oblique nod to P. D. James through Paretsky's naming of the news photographer who helps V. I. "Cordelia Hull."

The title of Paretsky's first novel, *Indemnity Only,* echoes while revising James M. Cain's 1936 *Double Indemnity.* Although certainly a "tough-guy writer," in Geoffrey O'Brien's term, Cain insisted he was not an imitator of Hammett and did so in terms that are enormously revealing:

I belong to no school, hard-boiled or otherwise, and I believe these so-called schools exist mainly in the imagination of critics. . . . If he can write a book at all, a writer cannot do it by peeping over his shoulder at anybody else, any more than a woman can have a baby by watching some other woman have one. It is a genital process. (preface to *The Butterfly,* quoted in O'Brien, pp. 71–72)

While entirely missing the point of literary influence, Cain's explicit linking of writing to the male role in sexual intercourse, with the pen a substitute penis, of course implies that women cannot write books (they have babies instead) as they lack the requisite equipment. This view of gender's influence on writing is not limited to the hard-boiled school of detective writers—a school to which Cain does belong, regardless of his refusal to wear its tie—but is, as Sandra Gilbert and Susan Gubar argue in *The Madwoman in the Attic*, "all pervasive in Western literary civilization" (p. 4). Gilbert and Gubar examine the metaphor of literary paternity, which they view as a "compensatory fiction" (p. 5), focusing on the "anxiety" the metaphor created in women who dared "attempt the pen" (p. 7) and pointing out that "a further implication of the paternity/creativity metaphor is the notion . . . that women exist only to be acted on by men, both as literary and as sensual objects" (p. 8). Hard-boiled detective fiction embraces the pen/penis equation, generally treating women as objects, and dangerous objects at that.

According to one critic, Dashiell Hammett's much-discussed bare style, especially his creation of a skeptical, tough voice for his detectives, represents the "voice of Male Experience," directly connected with male sexuality and with fantasies of male power (Naremore, p. 51). This critic admits that the pen seems to be a substitute penis for Hammett, pointing out that women in Hammett's books are always depicted as the "other" "to a central male consciousness" (Naremore, p. 52). In both Hammett's and Chandler's novels, women are usually amoral or predatory, with Chandler's heroes in particular exhibiting repugnance amounting to horror toward women's sexuality (Naremore, p. 52; Arden, p. 79; Grella, p. 109). In *The Big Sleep*, Philip Marlowe says, "I hate women," a statement he proves by slashing his bed after a woman has lain in it, hoping to seduce him; Mike Hammer, like Marlowe before him, takes pleasure in hitting women;[7] Sam Spade turns Brigid over to the police; James Cain makes Cora responsible for everything that happens in *The Postman Always Rings Twice*. Clearly, Paretsky's, Grafton's, Cody's, James's, and Muller's female heroes do not speak in the voice of male experience, nor do these novels posit woman as "other"—or, at least, not often. If the pen is not a substitute penis for these women, what is it? And what effect does the pen/penis equation have on their writing, if any?

One way to begin answering these questions is to examine some of the authors' treatments of another phallic substitute and staple of hard-boiled detective fiction, the gun. V. I. Warshawski buys a gun for self-protection in *Indemnity Only*, reasoning that she is at a disadvantage in facing armed thugs while herself un-armed. She knows how to use a gun, having been taught by her father, and recognizes while remaining suspect of the power guns embody. The difference between V. I. and those enamored of guns is succinctly summed up in her taunting of a hired thug who has beaten her up and wants to shoot her: "You big he-men really impress the shit out of me. . . . Why do you think the boy carries a gun? He can't get it up, never could, so he has a big old penis he carries around in his hand" (p. 203). Both Grafton's Kinsey Mill-hone and Marcia Muller's Sharon McCone are licensed to carry guns, but seldom do, preferring not to provoke violence. Sharon McCone's single use of her gun involves her shooting an armed man, one who is about to kill her best friend, and the shooting causes her to feel close to collapse. The first time Kinsey uses her gun, strictly in self-defense, she kills a man who is trying to kill her, and the shooting haunts her: "The shooting disturbs me still. It has moved me into the same camp with soldiers and ma-niacs. . . . I'll be ready for business again in a week or two, but I'll never be the same" (*"A" Is for Alibi* [1982], p. 215). Grafton has Kinsey use the gun again in *"E" is for Evidence* (1988), also in self-defense, but this time the gun does not help her, as shots seem only to energize her Rasputin-like attacker. Kinsey's hand-bag and a toilet tank lid prove to be better defensive weapons than the gun. The most interesting treatment of the female detective's use of a gun is P. D. James's *An Unsuitable Job for a Woman* (1972), wherein Cordelia Gray inherits a gun from her partner, Bernie Pryde, after his suicide. Cordelia "had never seen [the gun] as a lethal weapon, perhaps because Bernie's boyishly naive obsession with it had reduced it to the impotence of a child's toy. . . . It had been his most prized possession" (pp. 14–15). Cordelia never fires the gun, but uses it twice, once to scare off a sexually threatening motorist (p. 216) and once, knowing "that she wouldn't fire," to attempt to capture a man who has tried to kill her (p. 213). The gun is, of course, a lethal weapon, and is finally used lethally by another woman. Cordelia cares about the gun only because Bernie treasured it, seeing it more as a relic of her pathetically ineffectual partner than as a weapon she might actually use against someone else. All four of these writers demystify the gun, moving it from the realm of the symbolic, where it signifies male power and control, to the actual. Some of the characters specify situations wherein they will use the gun (only to save themselves or a friend), but Cordelia refuses ever to fire her gun, never wanting to assign to herself the power to reduce another human being to a thing. In these series, the gun ceases to be an exclusively phallic symbol, becoming something that can be wielded by either women or men, that can be used responsibly or irresponsibly.

The pen undergoes a similar transformation, becoming a gender-neutral tool available to both sexes. Speaking of nineteenth-century women writers, Gilbert and Gubar say that because "both patriarchy and its texts subordinate and imprison women, before women can even attempt that pen which is so rigorously kept from them they must escape just those male texts which, defining them as 'Cyphers,' deny them the autonomy to formulate alternatives to the authority that has imprisoned them and kept them from attempting the pen" (p. 13). In contrast to their sisters in the nineteenth century, contemporary women writers have access to a female tradition of authorship that offers numerous examples of women writers who have performed the necessary murder of the twinned images of woman as "other," the angel and the monster (Gilbert and Gubar, pp. 17–20); however, women creators of professional private detectives also have to deal in some way with the aggressively masculine, patriarchal tradition of the hard-boiled detective that posits woman as dangerous, destructive "other." Josephine Donovan, in "Toward a Women's Poetics," suggests that the woman writer cannot destroy the images and conventions that silence her if she works in isolation. Instead, "for the silenced Other to begin to speak, to create art, she must be in communication with others of her group in order that a collective 'social construction of reality' be articulated. Other social witnesses from the oppressed group must express their views, to validate one's own truth, that one may name it" (p. 101). All of the women writers considered in this chapter are "in communication with others of [their] group": as coparticipants in the social project of feminism, as readers of other women writers' work, and often in more intense involvements as well. Sara Paretsky, for instance, is active in the women's caucus of the Mystery Writers of America, criticizing the male domination of that group as expressed in the ratio of women to men nominees for awards.[8] The acknowledgments and dedication pages of several of these writers' books hint at a sort of community of women crime novelists: Marcia Muller dedicates *Ask the Cards a Question* to Sue Dunlap, author of the Jill Smith and Vejay Haskell series (discussed in chapters 4 and 2, respectively) and Sue Grafton thanks Marcia Muller in *"B" is for Burglar.* The voices that speak in these books are the voices of female experience, with the narratives often examining the effect on women of a masculinist construction of reality that describes woman as "other."

Although the fictional professional private eye, and especially the hard-boiled variety, seems an essentially American creation, the female version was born in England, with P. D. James's invention of Cordelia Gray; the first American woman private eye came along five years later in Marcia Muller's *Edwin of the Iron Shoes.* This transatlantic cross-fertilization invites speculation. Until quite recently, American literature, especially American fiction, seemed to represent a fairly coherent tradition, largely celebrating the solitary, individualistic hero who struck off into the wilderness in defiance of a restraining, feminizing social code.[9] The hard-boiled detective novel fits neatly within that tradition, with the private eye a (somewhat) updated version of what George Grella calls the "archetypal American hero," Natty Bumppo (p. 106); the male private eye shares Leatherstocking's remarkable physical abilities, his outsider status, and his isolation from most ordinary human relationships (Grella, p. 106). If this is *the* tradition, there is no room for women in it, as Peter O'Donnell and Arthur Kaplan proved with their offensive, ludicrous, only nominally female private eyes, Modesty Blaise and Charity Bay.[10]

The English crime novel tradition, on the other hand, at least included a goodly number of women writers and women characters, although most women authors chose male protagonists. P. D. James, whose main series character is Adam Dalgliesh, has said that she greatly admires Jane Austen and acknowledges both Dorothy Sayers and Margery Allingham as influences on her work (Joyner, pp. 110–11); she has also read at least some of the Amanda Cross novels (Bargainnier, p. 3). In temporarily abandoning the Dalgliesh series to write the first Cordelia Gray novel, James drew on these influences, most importantly on Jane Austen's compelling depictions of intelligent, resourceful young women coming to maturity in a society that asserted the only suitable destiny for a woman to be marriage and motherhood. Like *Emma,* the Austen novel James is said to admire most (Joyner, p. 111), *An Unsuitable Job for a Woman* follows a Bildungsroman pattern (Bakerman, p. 103); more importantly, as in Jane Austen's novels, the adult guides Cordelia encounters along her journey to adulthood are all negative examples, teaching Cordelia "what not to be" (Bakerman, pp. 109–10). Admittedly I am simplifying what is undoubtedly an infinitely complex process, but in outline what James does is adapt a preexisting, distinctively female pattern to a revised version of the imported hard-boiled detective novel, laying the groundwork for future women writers. Most of the other novels featuring female private eyes were published between 1982 and 1987 in the US. If James is one of the most important literary influences—showing in *An Unsuitable Job for a Woman* what could be done—then surely the pervasiveness of feminist thought and the increasing number of women's novels to be published are also contributors to the project of revising the hard-boiled genre.

James opened up the question of what the world might look like to a woman working as a professional investigator, and the novelists who have entertained that question in the intervening sixteen years have come up with surprisingly similar answers. All of the women private eyes meet male resistance in their work, a resistance brilliantly conveyed in the title of James's first Cordelia Gray novel. Cordelia is told several times that she is in the wrong line of work, that she is doing "an unsuitable job for a woman."

The "unsuitability" of the job lies in its requirements of action and of decision making, and in its placement of Cordelia in a position of independence and control, all suitable for a man but not for a woman. Whereas the male hard-boiled detectives are usually up against the widespread, generalized corruption of an entire society, with that corruption becoming particularized in the physical endangering of the detective, the women private eyes must face not only that widespread corruption and physical danger, but also specific hostility to women that frequently sharpens into personal attacks on the detective. Although all of the women detectives, like their male counterparts, see themselves as professionals, doing a job they have chosen, they must constantly overcome obstacles to doing that job that are specifically related to gender before they can tackle the obstacles the job itself entails; in other words, these women private eyes must repeatedly reestablish their right even to engage in the detective's struggle against evil. Misogyny may sometimes make it actually impossible for the detective to do her job at all, as is the case in Liza Cody's most recent Anna Lee novel, *Under Contract* (1986), wherein Anna's male colleagues from a larger firm, J. W. Security, continually undermine her efforts, refuse to listen to her theories about the case, and present more problems than does the rock star they are all supposed to be guarding. Cody does a marvelous job in *Under Contract* of making the reader feel the effects of sexual harassment, as the reader witnesses the unremitting tirade of insulting sexual remarks to which Anna is subjected and follows her increasing sense of isolation: this is what it means to be treated as an object.

Whereas the treatment of women as objects in male hard-boiled detective fiction results in a simple, clear pattern—women are all potentially destructive and predatory, with some women redeemed by their willingness to submit to patriarchal rule—women's private-eye novels encode no simple reversal of this pattern. Indeed, there is no pattern at all, or at least no single pattern, in these novels' depiction of either men or women. By removing women from the position of "other," these novelists open up an enormous range of possibilities for portraying women. That said, it is true that several of these novelists depict male-identified women as dangerous, marking as a threat

precisely the kind of woman exempted from threatening potentiality by the male novelists. In Paretsky's *Killing Orders,* for instance, the total dedication of several patriarchal women to the
system that deprives them of real power leads them to serve as
accomplices to murder; most horrifyingly, one such woman is an
accessory to her own daughter's death, representing in fiction
the feminist analysis that women who ally themselves with the
patriarchy destroy their own and their daughters'—actual and
metaphoric—life chances. In the novel's most chilling scene, V. I.
comes across this woman sitting in an attitude of attentive waiting
and realizes she is listening for the sound of the shot she expects
to end V. I.'s life. Liza Cody's two female villains—in *Head Case*
and *Under Contract*—act in service to patriarchal requirements;
one kills in order to maintain her social image as good, middle-
class wife, fearful that her adultery will be revealed and shatter
that facade. The other, a more complicated case because of her
lesbian relationship with a woman she actually hopes to destroy,
acts on her father's orders as an enforcer of her family's mob-style
"ownership" of a rock star.

As the preceding paragraph might suggest, marriage and the
family figure largely in a number of the novels featuring female
private eyes, a thematic dominance that appears to result from the
intersection and conflict of several competing ideological systems.
The male hard-boiled detective is defined by his isolation, his
complete lack of ordinary human relationships, with his status as
loner indicating both his separateness from the corrupt society his
tales indict and his descent from the romantic hero of quest tales
(Grella, p. 104).[11] The depiction of the male detective as a loner
links him with a long literary tradition of heroes in canonical
Western literature.[12] Women have generally been assigned to the
domestic sphere and defined by their relationships to others, particularly to family members, with the female loner seldom seen
as a hero in literature or in life.[13] The family is, of course, often
the locus of women's oppression, with traditional family arrangements mirroring social arrangements under patriarchy and
making the continuation of those social arrangements possible.
Nancy Chodorow, Dorothy Dinnerstein, and Adrienne Rich,
in now widely known books,[14] have analyzed the psychological

effects on both sexes of traditional family arrangements in which the mother is the primary caretaker and the father the link to the public world. Chodorow's theory, perhaps currently the most influential feminist account of human psychology, posits that whereas boys learn to define themselves in opposition to the mother, with separation and individuation central tasks, girls' identities develop in terms of identification and symbiosis with the mother, with this early bonding influencing women later to seek replications of the experience of interdependence and deep connectedness. It is no simple matter, then, for adult women to adopt a stance of separateness, and one might expect the female private detectives created by women to be less loners than their masculine counterparts, or at least to question the value of such isolation and to seek some form of connection with others.

All five novelists begin by deliberately establishing their female heroes as cut off from their families of origin, with Liza Cody's Anna Lee and Marcia Muller's Sharon McCone estranged from their families, who cannot accept or understand the women's choice of careers and life-styles, and Grafton's Kinsey Millhone, Paretsky's V. I. Warshawski, and James's Cordelia Gray all orphans. Grafton's hero has been orphaned twice: raised by a wonderfully unconventional aunt after her parents' deaths in a car crash when she was seven, Kinsey was left completely without family when that aunt died ten years before the events of *"A" is for Alibi*. Both of V. I.'s parents are dead at the commencement of Paretsky's series, as are Cordelia's in *An Unsuitable Job for a Woman*, where we learn that Cordelia's father died only recently, but she was raised as if she were an orphan: her mother died in childbirth, and her father left her to a series of foster homes and boarding schools until she was an adult. None of the five detectives is married, although Grafton's hero has been twice divorced and Paretsky's once; their single status suggests some resistance to the societal demand that women forsake their primary attachment to the mother and instead seek out a male love object.[15] Perhaps even more significantly, none of these detectives is herself a mother, although V. I. Warshawski often wonders what having a child might be like.

In their solitariness—parentless, spouseless, childless—these characters resemble the male hard-boiled detectives, but the resemblance is a superficial one that makes deeper differences all the more striking. In every one of the novels in these five series, the female hero is shown both to relish her independence and to seek intimate connections with others; however, for that cherished independence to be preserved, the connections must fall outside the boundaries of those socially sanctioned relationships that have defined and oppressed women. The women authors portray their heroes as freely but carefully choosing important relationships that do not merely replicate traditional ones—essentially inventing new modes of connectedness. Unsurprisingly, each of the heroes experiences the greatest difficulty in breaking free of the codes governing heterosexual relationships, with sexual involvement with a man always posing a threat to her independence, as the man eventually either perceives the detective's commitment to her job as an obstacle to be overcome or asserts his need to protect her in some fashion.

Only Muller creates a relatively conflict-free romantic relationship for her detective, as the three most recent Sharon McCone novels—*Games to Keep the Dark Away* (1984), *Leave a Message for Willie* (1984), and *There's Nothing to Be Afraid Of* (1985)—incorporate subplots following Sharon's involvement with a disc jockey who is a near paragon of feminist manhood: he really listens to women, respects Sharon's commitment to her job, never expects that theirs will be a traditional relationship, etc. In *Leave a Message for Willie,* Sharon worries that Don will be like other men in her past who have hated her job and then that his moving to San Francisco, where she lives, will doom their relationship: "It seemed to me that relationships between men and women didn't last very long these days. And it also seemed that, the more you were together, the more you hastened that almost certain end" (p. 77). Over time, Don proves himself to be unlike other men Sharon has known, with his differences finally persuading her that their relationship might last. Nevertheless, even this character ultimately interferes with Sharon's work on a case, blundering into a very delicate and dangerous situation because, he tells her, "I couldn't just sit there, knowing you might be in danger"

(*Nothing,* p. 186). Although Sharon claims to be furious with him—"I wanted to scream at him. I wanted to hurl the gun at his head" (p. 186)—she quickly forgives him, and they strike a deal, each agreeing to stick to his or her own turf. Muller is more interested in providing her detective with an ongoing sexual relationship than are the other writers discussed here,[16] but far less interested in seriously exploring the ramifications of gender-based conflict within personal relationships than are Cody, Paretsky, and Grafton.

An enduringly popular axiom of the women's movement—"the personal is political"—provides an essential insight into feminist analyses of heterosexual relationships generally and, especially, into the institutions of marriage and the family. If, as I asserted earlier, the family has traditionally been women's primary reality and the locus of oppression, then all legal improvements in women's status mean very little without a fundamental reimagining and reordering of women's position within the family and within other "personal" relationships. Private heterosexual relationships, then, must be seen as one highly important battleground in the struggle for women's liberation[17] as other advances into a feminist future finally turn on a widespread revolution in women's roles within those relationships. Several novels by Cody, Grafton, and Paretsky draw attention to the difficulty of this task, considering the deeply ingrained social assumptions that militate against truly egalitarian relations between men and women. Virtually every man with whom these detectives become involved tries to change them in some way or reveals unexamined sexist assumptions once the relationship is under way, after a period of good behavior when he tries to establish his supposed respect for her work. This pattern of buried assumptions rising to the surface reminds me of a colleague's student, who let slip some outrageous remark and then said, quite seriously, "I'm not really a sexist; I just forgot not to be."

Most often, these assumptions surface when the detective sees her work as more important than a social engagement and the man objects, believing their relationship should take precedence over work in the woman's life, but not necessarily in his own. V. I. Warshawski identifies such an incident as the moment she recognized that her marriage was irretrievably damaged (*Indemnity Only*, pp. 141–42), telling a new lover that her ex-husband "thought he'd fallen in love with me because I'm so independent; afterwards it seemed to me that it was because he saw my independence as a challenge, and when he couldn't break it down, he got angry" (p. 141). In *Bad Company* (1982), Anna Lee takes a fairly mild criticism by a new lover as a danger signal, thinking "sadly that a man who really liked her would not be so quick to try and change her" (p. 14), a comment that turns out to be prescient, since that first criticism opens the way to more serious ones, culminating in the man's insistence that she not work on a weekend he wants to spend sailing. Although he quickly realizes the absurdity of his final comment ("You're never around when I'm free. Look, I'm not possessive, but either you're my woman or you're not," [p. 51]), and bursts out laughing, the demand that Anna make his wishes central in her life is a serious one. Their relationship ends when he evidently realizes Anna will not capitulate to his demands and he finds a more pliant woman.

In Cody's next novel, *Stalker* (1984), Anna becomes involved with a man who appears to her to be ideal, but her friend Selwyn warns her, "He's too bloody forceful by half. . . . You mark my words. You're no match for him, Leo. He's already got you dancing to his tune" (p. 150). Anna ignores Selwyn's warning and her own doubts, allowing her infatuation with Ian Olsen to blind her to potential problems:

> If she had been asked, she would have said that she was too busy to ask herself questions. The days were too hectic and the nights too joyous. She was trained to ask questions, and it was one of her firm beliefs that acting blindly, when there was sufficient information to be had for the asking, was foolish and in the end self-defeating. Professionally, she understood that to stop asking questions when she had enough information to satisfy herself was also dangerous.
>
> But like so many professional people, she did not apply professional standards to private matters. (pp. 152–53)

Anna's involvement with Ian intensifies after her boss forces her to take some leave time when a case she is working on first becomes dangerous and then is shelved. The relationship itself seems like a vacation from Anna's real life, with Anna temporarily immersing herself in Ian's wealthier, more high-powered world, even moving into his flat and taking on the job of redecorating it to suit Ian. This period comes to an unhappy end, though, as Ian's wife decides not to divorce him after all and Anna learns that Ian expects her to fight his wife for him in what he admits is a game (p. 169), acknowledging the truth of Anna's sarcastic description of the triangle as "some kind of wanting contest" in which Ian will "go to the highest bidder without showing any preference of [his] own" (p. 168). This is the same old game of male dominance, but with a new twist: Ian places himself in the powerful position by refusing to acknowledge need or desire, leaving the women to expose their neediness and dependence and awarding himself to the most needy. Anna refuses to play, leaving Ian and returning to the familiar world of work the next day.

Like Paretsky's and Cody's detectives, Sue Grafton's Kinsey Millhone encounters as many problems in personal relationships with men as she does in professional ones; unlike the former two, though, Kinsey does not usually suspend her doubts in order to become involved with men, seeing sexual relationships as risky. In the first book of the Millhone series, "A" is for Alibi, the dangers of the job and those of heterosexual relationships merge, as Kinsey has an affair with the man she ultimately realizes is the killer for whom she is searching. When first attracted to him, Kinsey compares the feeling to a suicidal impulse: "It's the same sensation I have sometimes on the twenty-first floor when I open a window— a terrible attraction to the notion of tumbling out. I go a long time between men and maybe it was time again" (p. 52). This man has already killed one woman and kills two more before attempting to murder Kinsey, so her early analogy is quite accurate: involvement with Scorsoni *is* suicidal. In some ways, "A" is for Alibi is very close to traditional hard-boiled stories, with a sex-role switch: the detective puts aside suspicions, becomes sexually involved with a person who turns out to be the killer, discovers the truth, and punishes the dangerous lover. Considered from this angle, *Alibi* fuses *The Maltese Falcon* with Mickey Spillane-style violence as Kinsey finally kills the man who duped her. However, the alteration in sex roles is not the only revision Grafton makes, as the novel's central theme is women's position in marriage, with Scorsoni's cool murdering of three people to cover his embezzling set against a woman's poisoning of the ex-husband who cruelly punished her for years. The crime of passion committed by the woman pales in comparison to the man's cold determination to destroy anyone who gets in his way. Kinsey's killing of this man is in self-defense and is further mitigated by the thematic context in which it occurs. Nevertheless, *Alibi* does come uncomfortably close to a mere reversal of hard-boiled conventions, with all the men in the novel potentially dangerous but all the women granted subjectivity and individuality, with their crimes and failings excused by their subordination to men.

The treatment of male-female relationships is more complex in the next three novels in the Millhone series, with none of these making the simplistic gender divisions of *Alibi*. Kinsey's experience with Scorsoni in that first novel, though, provides an important context for her unwillingness to take risks with men in the next three books; in *"B" is for Burglar* Kinsey finds herself deeply attracted to a man but does not act on that attraction until *"D" is for Deadbeat* (1987), when she finally overcomes her "bone deep caution," deciding that she is usually too "careful not to make mistakes. Sometimes I wonder what the difference is between being cautious and being dead" (pp. 174–75). Even the involvements with men Kinsey does allow herself are more physical than emotional; she says in *"C" is for Corpse* "I like my life just as it is" (p. 13), and any deep emotional entanglement would inevitably change that life in some way. She sees her sexual relationships as following a cyclical rhythm:

About every six or eight months, I run into a man who astounds me sexually, but between escapades, I'm celibate, which I don't think is any big deal. After two unsuccessful marriages, I find myself keeping my guard up, along with my underpants. (p. 13)

With the exception of Marcia Muller, none of these authors show their detectives' emotional needs being met by their sexual relationships with men; instead, most of the detectives' deepest commitments are to what I would characterize as "chosen families."

Kinsey Millhone, for instance, has important relationships with her landlord, Henry Pitts, who lives in the main house on the property where her one-room apartment, a converted garage, is located,[18] and with Rosie, the proprietor of a rather seedy neighborhood bar. Both of these characters are more than twice Kinsey's age and may at first seem to fit neatly into the roles of substitute father and mother, but that would be a gross oversimplification of their function. Each does fulfill a few of the traditional requirements of parents, with Henry worrying about Kinsey's safety and Rosie providing food, but their roles in Kinsey's life do not fit into any established patterns. Neither exerts—or attempts to exert—the kind of power over Kinsey generally wielded by parents over children and neither stays within sex-role boundaries (Henry also bakes bread, for instance, while Rosie offers advice on a case). Most importantly, Kinsey's relationship with each is an egalitarian one, with both Henry and Rosie respecting her independence and professional competence. In *"E" is for Evidence* Grafton dramatizes the significance of chosen families and their superiority to the nuclear variety by enmeshing Kinsey in a case that turns on ugly family secrets. With Rosie and Henry both out of town for the Christmas holidays, Kinsey at first feels alone and lonely, cut off from the special warmth and affection she imagines siblings share. The more Kinsey learns about the Wood family, though, the more she values her freedom to choose her relatives, so to speak, and the more she appreciates the life she has fashioned for herself.

The setting Cody creates for Anna Lee may superficially resemble a substitute nuclear family, with her downstairs neighbors Bea and Selwyn Price acting as Anna's parents, but the resemblance is only superficial. Bea and Selwyn look out for Anna Lee's interests, often feed her, and frequently offer their advice on matters both personal and professional; however, the roles in this relationship are fluid, with Anna also looking out for Bea and Selwyn, providing food, and offering advice. Like Grafton's hero's relationships with Henry and Rosie, Anna's with Bea and Selwyn are egalitarian. Paretsky shows V. I.'s most important relationship to be with Lotty Herschel, an older woman who tells the detective she is "the daughter I never had . . . as well as one of the best friends a woman could ever desire" (*Killing,* p. 276). Their relationship comes close to replicating the mother-daughter bond, but, as Lotty's comments suggests, is not simply or exclusively a mother-daughter one. V. I. has other important women friends as well, but few men friends, which she explains is "because I don't feel they're [women] trying to take over my turf. But with men, it always seems, or often seems, as though I'm having to fight to maintain who I am" (*Indemnity Only,* p. 141). In *Bitter Medicine* (1987), V. I. gets close to an older man who wants to play father to her, but she is able to work out the limits of their relationship with him, sometimes calling on him for help and sometimes aiding him, in the sort of easy give-and-take characteristic of good friendships.

Cordelia Gray is the most solitary of all the women detectives, but James depicts that solitariness not as a cynical turning away from human companionship but as a result of youth and of background. Cordelia is only twenty-two in *An Unsuitable Job for a Woman* and used to doing most of her living inside her own head as the result of a childhood and adolescence spent without privacy but also without genuine intimacy. During the course of that novel Cordelia begins to establish relationships with others; her most intense involvement, however, is with a dead young man. Investigating the circumstances of Mark's death, Cordelia moves into his cottage, gets to know his friends, wears his clothes, and very nearly becomes him, an identification further emphasized by her coming close to being murdered, as he was. Apart from this intimacy with the spirit of Mark Callendar—a feat of imagination comparable to Cordelia's earlier fantasizing of a bond established with her mother in the brief interval between her birth and her mother's death: "In her imagination she had enjoyed a lifetime of love in one hour with no disappointments and no regrets" (*Unsuitable,* p. 21)—Cordelia resists intimacy, apparently thinking friendships might interfere with the job she is just learning to do. Cordelia's comparative youth is an important factor. The other detectives discussed here are about ten years older than Cordelia, their professional competence and personal independence a given as the series featuring them begin, with Muller, Cody, Paretsky, and Grafton focusing on the crises of maturity.

James, in contrast, interests herself in the personality traits and personal experiences that might enable a young woman to become a self-sufficient adult and a self-assured professional (Campbell, p. 499). As Jane Bakerman demonstrates, *An Unsuitable Job for a Woman* is a modern feminist Bildungsroman centered on a protagonist who defeats the system she has come to know through her trials (pp. 104–5). Bakerman emphasizes the importance of autonomy in *An Unsuitable Job for a Woman* (p. 106), but the second Cordelia Gray novel, *The Skull beneath the Skin* (1982), suggests that autonomy is just one stage along the road to maturity and that the next stage involves risking that autonomy for the sake of relatedness. *Unsuitable* hints at this movement toward connections with others when Cordelia decides to make Ronald Callendar's death look like a suicide so that Miss Leaming will not be arrested: "They [Cordelia and Miss Leaming] had nothing in common except their sex, although Cordelia had realized . . . the strength of that female allegiance " (p. 264). This is Cordelia's first acknowledgment of a bond with the living; it is especially important to note that this first bond is with a group, not with an individual. Cordelia establishes her professional competence by holding herself entirely apart from others; that competence established, she begins to move back into the world by accepting herself as part of a particular social group, women. The next step, which Cordelia takes in *Skull*, is to choose relationships with particular, living people; the first bonds Cordelia chooses are with employees, for whom she feels a certain responsibility and relationships with whom she can control. As *Skull* progresses, though, Cordelia opens herself to less structured, less safe relationships, and to all the potential for pain they involve. At the end of the novel she reflects that animals are easier to deal with than are people,[19] but it is clear that she plans no retreat from the complexities of human relationships.

Much in the way that they revise hard-boiled fiction's insistence on the isolation of the hero, so do women writers revise the meaning of violence. Placing the hero in physical danger is a convention of the genre (Naremore, p. 55), but a convention whose meaning is entirely changed when the detective is a woman. A male detective who uses his wits and his fists to fight his way out of a dangerous situation is acting within gender role expectations, but a woman who performs the same feat is not; whereas the male detective proves his masculinity through bloodying his opponents and emerging triumphant from the contest, a woman doing the same thing calls her femininity into question. The extreme violence of male hard-boiled detective fiction respects genre requirements, catering to the readers of pulp magazines, but the lesser violence of women's detective fiction does not merely mimic male models. Hard-boiled characters glory in violence, and it comes naturally to them, but their female counterparts have more mixed emotions, most clearly visible in a passage from Paretsky's *Killing Orders,* where V. I. traps a man who has tried to kill her. She shoots him in the leg and then tries to "force down the desire to kill [him] where he lay" (p. 236). After she threatens to shoot him again if he does not answer her questions, the man says, "You wouldn't" and V. I. thinks:

He was probably right; my stomach was churning as it was. What kind of person kneels in the snow threatening to destroy the leg of an injured man? Not anyone I wanted to know. I pulled the hammer back with a loud click and pointed the gun at his left leg. (p. 237)

This brief reflection is a striking record of ambivalence: she thinks she will not shoot him because she is sickened by the first shot, wonders what she has become, feels she does not even want to know the self who behaves so violently, and then goes on with the threat, perhaps even willing to carry it out. None of the women detectives usually takes pleasure in violence and none initiates it, as the male detectives often do; however, these books suggest that violence may sometimes be the only possible response to a violent milieu and all of the detectives are able to hold their own in a fight. These women refuse the conventionally feminine role of victim, fighting back against those who would victimize them and thereby preserving themselves. None of the women ever needs rescuing; each rescues herself from danger. The frequency with which women authors invent scenes in which the female detective uses her intelligence and her physical strength to overcome a violent threat suggests that they see such scenes as important refutations of the stereotypes of women be-coming distraught under pressure, being the weaker sex both emotionally and physically, and requiring male protection.

Liza Cody's *Bad Company* most searchingly explores the mean-ing of a woman's fighting back, suggesting wider application of Anna Lee's behavior. Early in the novel, Anna witnesses a group of men grabbing a teenage girl, intervenes to help the girl, and knocks off one thug's motorcycle helmet, consequently making it possible for her to identify him and imperative that he kidnap her as well as the girl to prevent Anna's going to the police. For 194 of the novel's 287 pages, Anna and the girl, Verity, are held cap-tive by the four thugs, in a literalization of women's enclosure and entrapment in society. Anna has been hit on the head and both captives are at first tied up. The two are kept in a dimly lit base-ment, with only an old iron bed, a burned mattress, and a slop bucket for furniture; their captors sometimes forget to bring them food and water or to empty the slop bucket.

From the first, Anna must fight not only against her captors but also against Verity, who objects to Anna's taking any kind of action for fear that their captors will mistreat them more; Verity clings to her role of good daughter, transferring the paternal part to her captors. Verity's theory of survival is actually widely shared by oppressed peoples, and goes something like this: if you do what the powerful tell you, never speak up against them, never assert yourself in any way, then you may win the protection and pity of those in power; fighting back, on the other hand, is sure to be self-defeating because the powerful by definition will always have more power than you and can make you even more miserable. Anna, older and wiser than Verity, knows that accepting power-lessness is death, and is determined to keep her spirit alive while hoping also to save the body that houses it. She demands food, argues with and mocks the kidnappers, tries to pick the lock on the room's door, and breaks a window to call for help, all while trying to protect the weaker Verity and countering Verity's self-centered complaints that Anna is "just making trouble . . . mak-ing them lose their temper. And it's me they'll take it out on in the end" (p. 133). Anna's dogged resistance results in better condi-tions for both of them, but even after their ordeal ends Verity persists in her good-girl philosophy, saying their captors "weren't too bad really" and obliquely criticizing Anna with the comment that "some people just don't deserve respect or good manners" (p. 274). *Bad Company* operates as an allegory of women's possible responses to oppression, with Anna's resistance and refusal to accept her captors' terms clearly the better part. The novel's conclusion is doubly ironic, as Anna and Verity are freed not through Anna's efforts or the efforts of the police and private investigators, but through a sort of fluke as the kidnappers' plans go awry and it is Verity, not Anna, who is lauded in the media. The terms of that praise are revealing, though: "A Brave Little Girl Wins Through" is the headline on one story.

I do not want to leave the impression here that all five female private eyes are morally pure heroes who resort to violence only in self-defense, as that is not exactly accurate. On the whole, these detectives eschew violence except when threatened with violence, but Paretsky's V. I. Warshawski occasionally takes some pleasure in beating up a male antagonist, which may reflect the author's delight in creating a woman character who so often triumphs where so few actual women do. Paretsky's *Killing Orders* takes this triumph further in a really shocking abuse of power by V. I. that the author seems not to judge harshly, or at all for that matter. V. I. approaches a Mafia don with information about an archbishop who has tried to have her killed and has had her friend Agnes killed. Knowing that the archbishop is beyond the reach of the law, V. I. passes the don information she realizes will result in the archbishop's assassination. In a scene that parallels the one mentioned earlier in this chapter, where V. I. comes across a woman listening for the shot that will end V. I.'s life, V. I. describes hearing "the sound I had been waiting for. A dull roar, an explosion muffled by distance and stone walls" (p. 273): the sound of the archbishop's car exploding, with a radio bomb placed by the Mafia. The rest of this scene suggests that one is to read the archbishop's death, and V. I.'s role in it, as simple justice, but troubling questions obtrude. What makes V. I. at all different from the Mafia don, the archbishop, or any other person who arrogates to him or her self the right to decide who lives and who dies? The ethical quagmire is worsened by V. I.'s finally accepting twenty-five thousand dollars from the same don, clearly meant as payment for services rendered; V. I. has acted, then, as a paid informant to the Mafia, abandoning the high moral ground she has earlier claimed for herself. At the end of *Killing Orders,* Paretsky comes very close to simply reinscribing the worldview encoded in male hard-boiled novels, but with the crucial revision that V. I. acts in accordance with no code at all and without reflection.

The male heroes of hard-boiled detective novels always act in accordance with their own moral codes (Grella, p. 107), which may be very far indeed from the dominant ideology or from legality. Dashiell Hammett's detectives, in particular, are not virtuous by any common definition of the term, and share with Raymond Chandler's a distrust of the police and a near hatred of the rich and their influence on the legal system (Arden, p. 80; Naremore, p. 51). The hard-boiled detective usually views the police as incompetent or corrupt (Grella, p. 106) and concerns himself with exposing this incompetence or corruption, along with the other kinds of falsehood he sets himself against (Naremore, p. 51). Female private eyes share some of these characteristics, with only Muller's novels incorporating a general respect for the police and for the legal system's ability to administer justice. Of course, Muller's hero works for that legal system, albeit for one of its less conventional arms: a legal coop that specializes in providing legal services to the poor. Anna Lee, like Sharon McCone but unlike the other three detectives, is not self-employed but works for a security firm whose owner maintains close professional contact with the police and as a consequence is herself often involved with the police. Cody's novels, however, unlike Muller's, tend to portray the police as self-serving, rather stupid,[20] even downright dangerous, easily violating others' rights as they single-mindedly go about their jobs.[21] The police are most negatively portrayed in the three series in which the heroes are given similar backgrounds: Cody's Anna Lee spent five years as a police officer before joining Brierly Security; Grafton's detective is an ex-cop who left the force after she realized her good guys/bad guys views were naïve, but soon turned to private investigation because she missed "the intermittent sick thrill of life on the edge" (*Burglar,* p. 1); Paretsky's V. I. Warshawski is a lawyer who quit the public defender's office when she became "disillusioned" by the "pretty corrupt" system in which "you're never arguing for justice, always on points of law" (*Indemnity Only,* p. 141). Paretsky, in particular, often portrays the inequities of the legal system, with all of her novels incorporating in some way the theme of the ability of the rich and powerful—big labor, big business, organized religion, the Mafia, big medicine—to manipulate the legal system, from the police to the courts to the lawmakers.

To varying degrees, all of the female detectives hold themselves apart from the legal system; none, however, usually sees herself as above the law or as a law unto herself as do some of the hard-boiled men, most notably Mickey Spillane's Mike Hammer. In fact, several—including V. I. Warshawski, except for the episode with the mob in *Killing Orders*—see themselves as defenders of the law, working to right wrongs and to provide justice in cases where the official system of justice has failed. V. I. finds in her "independent professional work" (*Indemnity,* pp. 36–37) the freedom to work for justice she sorely missed as a public defender; asked to talk about her job in *Killing Orders,* she speaks in terms of freedom and justice:

I guess the payoff is you get to be your own boss. And you have the satisfaction of solving problems, even if they're only little problems most of the time. . . . [As public defenders] either we had to defend maniacs who ought to have been behind bars for the good of the world at large, or we had poor chumps who were caught in the system and couldn't buy their way out. You'd leave court every day feeling as though you'd just helped worsen the situation. As a detective, if I can get at the truth of a problem, I feel as though I've made some contribution. (p. 77)

V. I.'s idea of justice is a familiar one, based on a liberal humanist belief in individual responsibility, but tempered by a concern for contexts and for details, and essentially separate from an ideal of order.

Sharon McCone and Kinsey Millhone think similarly to V. I., with Kinsey articulating her theory of justice in *"A" is for Alibi* as she compares two cases she has been working on, one a murder and the other an insurance scam:

I thought about Gwen [the murderer] without surprise or dismay, my mind jumping forward and back randomly. Somehow I was more offended by the minor crimes of a Marcia Threadgill who tried for less, without any motivation at all beyond greed. I wondered if Marcia Threadgill was the new standard of morality against which I would now judge all other sins. Hatred, I could understand—the need for revenge, the payment of old debts. That's what the notion of "justice" was all about anyway: settling up. (p. 192)

This idea of justice as "settling up" is obviously a fairly primitive one, but one also rooted in a concern for relationships and for life. Kinsey never perceives people as owing some kind of debt to the abstraction of society, but does believe people owe debts to other people. *"D" is for Deadbeat* is about this concept of justice, with many of Grafton's characters trying to pay the debts they believe they owe those they have hurt and others trying to exact such payment for wrongs they have suffered. The book ends with Kinsey unsuccessfully trying to talk the murderer—a fifteen-year-old boy who killed the man responsible for his parents' and sister's deaths—out of suicide, telling him that he deserves to get away with this murder. Although this scene suggests that the one debt one can never owe is one's own life, the postscript challenges that implication, with Kinsey speculating that the boy's victim may have felt he owed the boy his life as a "sacrifice": "Some debts of the human soul are so enormous only life itself is sufficient forfeit" (p. 229).

In contrast to the hard-boiled male detectives, none of the female private eyes adheres to a hard-and-fast moral code, with this difference between the two groups similar to the gender differences in moral reasoning Carol Gilligan explores in *In a Different Voice.* The two most interesting examples of women's moral decision making come from the British authors, Liza Cody and P. D. James. Cody has Anna, in *Bad Company,* break the rules of client privilege in order to warn a woman that her ex-husband is having her investigated in hopes of obtaining custody of their daughter. Although she does not know the woman, Anna is repelled by the ex-husband, her firm's former client, who is a fanatic conservative. Anna knows she could lose her job for speaking with this woman and after their talk she "felt she had been thoroughly unprofessional, but at least she had made some attempt to redeem" the woman's daughter and she now has "a much lighter heart" (p. 287). Anna here acts on some sense of female solidarity, much as Cordelia Gray does when she covers up the evidence of Miss Leaming's crime. Adam Dalgliesh, who suspects the truth, tries to get Cordelia to confess, running through her possible motives for lying, which he decides are basically two: to protect herself or to protect someone else, with the motive for the latter being "love, fear, or a sense of justice." He decides justice is the most likely because Cordelia does not seem "very easy to frighten" nor does he think she could love any of the people involved, having known them for such a short time (p. 275). Dalgliesh for once is wrong, as the reader knows from Cordelia's earlier conversation with Miss Leaming, who tells her, "I thought you might have acted in the service of justice or some such abstraction" (p. 257), to which Cordelia responds, "I wasn't thinking about any abstraction. I was thinking about a person" (p. 258). The person is not Miss Leaming as Miss Leaming, but Miss Leaming as the mother of Mark (p. 237), the dead boy to whom Cordelia has come to feel close; Cordelia's motive is love, both in particular and in the abstract, as her earlier, passionate defense of love as a guide to and reason for living makes clear (pp. 226–27). Cordelia's and Anna's choices reflect their relative lack of concern with abstractions or with absolutes and their tendency to think contextually, a mode of thinking Gilligan finds characteristic of women, who tend to perceive moral problems as problems of relationships, with morality lying in "recognizing connection" and absolute judgments "yield[ing] to the complexity of relationships" (p. 59).

Gilligan's construction of women's moral decision making is based on Chodorow's analysis of female psychology, in which the female child's early bonding with the mother is perceived as such an intense and pleasurable sensation that women go through life seeking replications of that experience and seeing ego boundaries as fluid, with autonomy far less important than intimate connections with others. The importance of the mother in several of the series discussed in this chapter can hardly be overstated. James has Cordelia sustain herself through that fantasy of the mother mentioned earlier, with Cordelia mentally consulting her imagined mother at several points in *An Unsuitable Job for a Woman*. Told by another woman that Cordelia's mother would certainly not think her job quite nice for a young woman, Cordelia conjures up the fantasy mother, who assures her that it is an eminently suitable job (p. 21). Estranged from her own mother, Anna Lee investigates cases that always return in some way to family and especially to the mother. Most of the mothers in Cody's novels are patriarchal, subservient to the father, but in the first novel of the series, *Dupe* (1981), Cody has Anna mistake a mother's silence for assent. When Anna learns that this woman is no dupe after all, but sees clearly what her child was yet continues to love her, Anna is forcibly reminded that not all mothers are alike. V. I. Warshawski romanticizes her dead mother Gabriella, who is a presence in every one of the Paretsky novels, most frequently entering the novels through the objects that represent her, a set of red Venetian glasses. V. I. has a lot invested in her image of her mother as all-loving, all-giving, yet her intuitive, half-buried recognition of her mother as a complex, flawed, real person—a subject, not an object—is sensitively indicated by Paretsky through the glasses, which are prized but fragile. V. I. tries to protect those glasses, as she tries to protect her childlike fantasy of her mother, but they are often endangered and two are broken during the series. At the end of *Killing Orders* V. I. recounts a dream in which her mother, who named her, takes Agamemnon's (the father's) part in the myth of Iphigenia, sacrificing V. I. to atone for her own sins. It seems to me that Paretsky might be moving V. I. toward a mature understanding of her mother, neither the ideal mother nor the deadly figure of the dream, and therefore toward a more complete sense of self.

Women authors of detective fiction speak in a voice different from the cynical, detached one typical of male creators of hard-boiled novels, with the protagonists of the novels reflecting this difference in myriad ways. Every feature of male hard-boiled detective novels is transformed in women's novels, with the detective's isolation or connectedness, attitude toward violence, sense of justice, and sense of self essentially different in male- and female-authored works. The only commonalities that remain are, for the most part, superficial: the tough talk from the detective, the taking notice of details of life like money, food, and clothing, the distrust of the police, and the occupation of the main character.

6

Lesbian Detectives

While speaking recently with a lesbian colleague about a planned conference, I was brought up short by her saying, in a tone that implied she was stating a widely accepted matter of fact, "I would have as much trouble with a straight woman talking about lesbian writers as with a white woman talking about black women's writing." Already late for class, I said I disagreed, but neither of us was able to pursue her argument at that moment, nor have we really returned to it. Perhaps because both of us are already weary of making the same old argument to yet another person, we seem to have agreed to disagree. There are of course many things that divide women— among them age, race, class, and sexual identity; I believe that attempts to bridge these differences are absolutely crucial to the survival of the feminist movement(s) and to the survival and flowering of each woman individually. Minimizing or ignoring differences will not make them go away, nor should we *want* them to go away, whereas emphasizing differences to the exclusion of all commonalities will only increase the distance between old and young, black, white, and Asian, working and middle-class, lesbian and heterosexual women. Straight women have to learn to listen to their lesbian sisters, to respect their voices, and to read their writing, just as white women must learn to pay that same kind of careful attention to women of color. While paying attention, though, they must also be certain that they do not mistake eradication of difference for inclusion of difference; in order to do that, they have to refuse the privileges of heterosexuality, skin color, class, or age, and to resist the temptation of the comparatively privileged to speak for anyone else. I am aware, then, that my reading of lesbian crime novels is inescapably the reading of a heterosexual woman and that a lesbian feminist analysis of these novels might well be very different from my own.[1] However, attempting some analysis, no matter how high the barriers, seems infinitely preferable to ignoring lesbian crime novels, as leaving them out of consideration, on whatever grounds, would be to participate in the silencing of their authors and therefore of all women.

Adrienne Rich, in "Compulsory Heterosexuality and Lesbian Existence," critiques several avowedly feminist books that ignore lesbian issues, showing that each book's failure to deal with "lesbian existence as a reality, and as a source of knowledge and power available to women" limits its accuracy, power, and influence (p. 141). Bonnie Zimmerman, in "What Has Never Been: An Overview of Lesbian Feminist Literary Criticism," begins by discussing the heterosexism,[2] "either by omission or by design," of feminist literary anthologies, women's studies journals, and feminist literary criticism (pp. 201–2), going on then to consider the recent work of lesbian feminist critics. According to Zimmerman, the two main tasks of lesbian feminist critics have been, and continue to be, establishing a lesbian canon, just as other feminist critics have worked on establishing a female canon, and articulating a lesbian critical perspective (pp. 203–4). This lesbian critical perspective is obviously unavailable to men or to straight women,[3] but it is possible to incorporate some of its methods, questions, and insights into a feminist criticism that sets itself against heterosexism, which is what I hope to do in this chapter. Zimmerman identifies the first question in developing a lesbian feminist perspective as "When is a text a 'lesbian' text or its writer a 'lesbian writer'?" (p. 204), pointing out that answering that question depends on the definition of *lesbian* with which one is working.[4] Competing definitions of *lesbian* and therefore of *lesbian writers* abound, ranging from Catherine Stimpson's purposefully narrow, carnal one in "Zero Degree Deviancy: The Lesbian Novel in

English" to Adrienne Rich's broad, inclusive idea of a lesbian continuum that covers a vast range of not necessarily carnal woman-identified experience ("Compulsory," pp. 156–57). For the purposes of this chapter, I will to some extent be following Lillian Faderman's definition, which lies about midway between Stimpson's and Rich's and which Zimmerman finds most helpful, of *lesbian* as describing an intense relationship between two women in which the women share "most aspects of their lives with each other" and in which there may be sexual contact (pp. 17–18). However, I also want to expand this definition to include any women—characters or authors—who identify themselves as lesbians, on whatever basis; it is also important to acknowledge, as Zimmerman does (p. 207), that Faderman's definition presupposes a monogamous relationship that does not adequately describe many lesbians' lives. To Faderman's definition and to my own expansion of it, I would add that there is an element of choice in lesbianism, as there is in bisexuality and heterosexuality, and that the choice has political ramifications that only heterosexual women can refuse to perceive. In most of the crime novels discussed in this chapter, the female hero does not experience her sexual and emotional attraction to women as an active, open choice she may make, but does perceive her acknowledgment of, and acting upon, that attraction as a matter of choice with strong political implications.

The process of accepting a lesbian identity is one thematic center of all the lesbian crime novels discussed here, with each novel concerning itself in some way with the implications of various kinds of "coming out": to oneself, to family, to friends, to potential lovers, to coworkers, and to the public generally. Several of these novels follow strikingly similar patterns, paralleling the hero's investigation of a crime or mystery with her investigation of her own psyche.[5] As the detective assembles the clues to the mystery, she also assembles the clues to her sexuality, with the revelation of the solution to the puzzle and the revelation of the detective's—or another major character's—lesbianism presented as complementary. Vicki McConnell's *Mrs. Porter's Letter* (1982) and Barbara Wilson's *Murder in the Collective* (1984) both treat lesbian awakenings as the female hero's recognition of her true self,[6] with both protagonists/narrators presenting themselves as heterosexual women recovering from broken love affairs with men as the novels open. McConnell's Nyla Wade is recently divorced and sometimes misses her ex-husband; subjected to the well-intentioned matchmaking efforts of her closest friend, Audrey Louise, Nyla resists, saying, "I'm generally not happy about what happens between men and women these days. I'm not sure how to remedy it. I'm not even sure it can be remedied. I just don't have anything to give again, not yet. And I'm not sure I want to anyway" (p. 42).[7] Nyla initially sees herself as a heterosexual woman who temporarily chooses celibacy. However, as the novel unfolds, Nyla's near obsession with a packet of love letters, her recurring vision of a scarlet flower she finds threatening, and her sexual attraction to a woman lead her to ask herself, "Does this mean I'm a Lesbian?" and to answer immediately, "Yes, I'm probably a Lesbian" (p. 162). Nyla does not act on her recognition until the next book in the series, *The Burnton Widows* (1984).

Wilson's Pam Nilsen describes herself as "estranged for ten months" from her male lover of three years, still feeling some regrets but not many serious ones (pp. 9–10); she is a bit homophobic, yet anxious to change, seeing a new lesbian member of the printing collective to which she belongs as probably "good for us [the collective] in the long run. She'd already opened my mind to a whole section of the community I'd never known very well before" (p. 11). Pam finds herself attracted to a lesbian, but initially denies that attraction:

At some point I would have to explain to Hadley that I was straight, not at all wavering, and that I didn't feel attracted to her, but just wanted her for a friend, even though I'd never had a lesbian friend before and had no idea if you even *could*. (p. 47)

Even after she admits to herself her sexual attraction to Hadley, Pam keeps avoiding making what she realizes is "a life-altering decision" (p. 73), at one point "working up" a "big speech" to give Hadley about "how I wasn't a lesbian, but I was sort of interested, but I didn't know, but I sort of wanted to find out, but I couldn't be sure, but I really liked her, but maybe just as a friend" (p. 101). As with McConnell's Nyla Wade, the reader knows before Pam does that she is in love with Hadley and that she is probably a lesbian. Eventually Pam acknowledges this love and acts on it, but continues to vacillate between seeing herself as a lesbian and as heterosexual for quite a while, with her sister's comment that "you're not gay with one . . . encounter" (p. 119) making good sense. As the second Pam Nilsen book, *Sisters of the Road* (1986), opens, though, Pam has accepted a lesbian identity that is not entirely dependent on one other woman (Hadley) or on *any* other woman, but is a matter of self-perception and self-definition.

Both heroes of McConnell's and Wilson's stories follow the lesbian Bildungsroman pattern Bonnie Zimmerman outlines in "Exiting from Patriarchy: The Lesbian Novel of Development":

the recognition of emotional and/or sexual feelings for another woman, the realization that that love is condemned by society, the acceptance of a lesbian identity either physically (through sexual initiation) or psychologically, and, in the contemporary feminist novels, the affirmation of one's lesbianism to the outside world. (p. 245)

Most of the other lesbian crime novels incorporate parts of this coming-out pattern, with the most complex being Valerie Miner's *Murder in the English Department* (1982). Miner's protagonist, Nan Weaver, feels an attachment and a responsibility to all women, evidenced by her deep commitment to several women's causes, and an especial attachment to her niece Lisa and to one of her students, Marjorie Adams. Nan protects Marjorie from a murder charge, thereby endangering herself: "it didn't make sense to defend Marjorie, yet Nan knew she was right" (p. 128). Although Nan and Marjorie have a rather cool, professional relationship that never becomes very intimate, and Nan, currently celibate (p. 33), implies heterosexuality, as when she imagines she might "reward that sweet fellow Claude for his committed but discreet pursuit these past six months" (p. 32), the strong hint of lesbianism or bisexuality toward the end of the novel comes as no surprise. When Nan, who has been jailed for murder, is released from prison, her family plans a party, which her sister describes as a "coming-out party" (p. 149):

Coming out, thought Nan. Perhaps it was time for that. If they had stood by her at the murder trial, maybe she could tell them about. . . . who knew what would come out next? (p. 149, ellipses in original)

Miner avoids labeling Nan either heterosexual or lesbian, but does draw attention to her choice of temporary celibacy, a choice that gives Nan the opportunity to focus on non-sexual relationships and to enjoy her own freedom. The brief acknowledgment of lesbian or bisexual identity is prepared for by Nan's deep commitment to feminist causes and intense emotional involvement with women. Miner seems to be working with a concept of lesbianism akin to Adrienne Rich's idea of a "lesbian continuum," with Nan's woman-identified experiences logically extending into the sexual or at least not ruling out the sexual. This treatment of sexuality may seem far indeed from the coming-out pattern Zimmerman describes, but there are some important parallels: Miner shows us Nan's "recognition of emotional and/or sexual feelings for another woman"; Nan, a professor of English who teaches women's studies, obviously knows that love for another woman "is condemned by society"; the coming-out musings quoted above both suggest Nan's "acceptance of a lesbian identity . . . psychologically" and imply that her "affirmation of [her] lesbianism to the outside world," as a component of her sexuality, lies in the not-too-distant future. Miner takes the lesbian crime novel beyond the coming-out pattern into a more complex realm where either/or choices do not suffice.

Several other lesbian detectives have been through the process Zimmerman identifies before the novels featuring them open—notably Sarah Dreher's eponymous hero of *Stoner McTavish* (1985) and Lauren Wright Douglas's Caitlin Reece of *The Always Anonymous Beast* (1987)—but become involved with women whose comings out are just beginning. Stoner, for example, falls in love with an apparently heterosexual, newly married woman who gradually awakens to, and acts on, her lesbian feelings,[8] while the case Caitlin investigates hinges on a supposedly straight woman's terror that her lesbian crush will be publicly exposed. Katherine V. Forrest's Kate Delafield of *Amateur City* (1984) has in one sense completed the coming-out process, but in another demonstrates the truth of Zimmerman's observation that this is an ongoing process that is never finished (p. 244), as the lesbian must constantly decide about coming out to new acquaintances and in a variety of circumstances. The process of coming out is most intriguingly worked out in Forrest's *Murder at the Nightwood Bar* (1987), where Kate weighs the conflicting requirements of her job as a police officer and of her obligations to herself as a lesbian and to other lesbians. Marion Foster, in *The Monarchs Are Flying* (1987), uses coming out doubly: one woman, a murder suspect, is stuck at the acceptance stage of coming out, unable to affirm her lesbianism to the outside world, while a second, a lawyer, is just beginning to recognize "emotional and/or sexual feelings" for the first woman. The lawyer helps the suspect, her client, to see her lesbianism as positive (in other words, to reject the social condemnation of lesbians) and to move toward public affirmation; in so doing, she explores her own attraction to this woman, a doubling of plot that is resolved singly in the novel's closing scene, which depicts the beginning of lovemaking between the two women. *The Monarchs Are Flying* fictionally recapitulates Zimmerman's point that "the end of the coming out process is freedom" (p. 246). Leslie Taylor is released from prison because Harriet, her lawyer, first helps her break out of the "prison of her own making" (p. 187); once Leslie stops hiding her lesbian identity, it cannot be used against her in quite the same way by those trying to convict her of murder. The closing lines of the novel explicitly link Harriet's discovery of her lesbianism to freedom:

Harriet closed her eyes and wondered, briefly, at the rightness of this moment and the years it had taken to reach it. She knew that she, like Leslie, was at last set free. (p. 217)

The freedom the coming-out process brings lies in self-acceptance, but is always countered in these novels—as it probably often is in life—by some restrictions of freedom in the outside world. Each coming out involves the woman's facing again the possibility of loss of community and, especially, of family. Fear of loss may be what keeps some characters silent, but the price of such silence is articulated by Douglas's Caitlin Reece and Marion Foster's Leslie Taylor. Caitlin remembers "my own years of obfuscating the truth. . . . I'd had precious little time to pursue romance, but still, the necessary lies were extremely tedious. I recalled being irked at the need to deceive my classmates or colleagues about who my dates *really* were" (p. 10), while Leslie has internalized her society's heterosexism and homophobia, seeing her lesbianism as "branding" her (p. 22) and describing the possibility of publicly acknowledging her sexual identity as being "put on exhibition like some freak in a side show" (p. 108). Despite her deep fears, Leslie's coming out does not result in the loss of her parents' love, which had been her overwhelming fear, yet exactly that withdrawal of love is often the price—or at least the *first* price—of coming out in lesbian crime novels. In *Stoner McTavish,* for instance, Dreher describes Stoner's parents as unwilling to accept their daughter's sexual identity or their daughter herself, responding to her coming out to them by trying to have her institutionalized. For Elena in *Murder in the Collective,* coming out was accompanied by a brutal custody battle with her ex-husband, while Dory Quillin in *Murder at the Nightwood Bar* was thrown out of her parents' house after coming out and cautioned never to contact them again.

Like the heterosexual women detectives discussed in chapter 5, most of the lesbian detectives are estranged or otherwise cut off from their families of origin and have established in families of choice. The authors of lesbian crime novels make the same criticisms of traditional families discussed in the preceding chapter—such families are oppressive to women and perpetuate the patriarchal power structure—but extend these criticisms into the particular oppression of the lesbian, ranging from silencing to physical abuse. Several of the lesbian detectives live in nontraditional arrangements, such as Stoner McTavish's housekeeping with her elderly, eccentric aunt and Pam Nilsen's collective household, which includes her sister and a heterosexual couple, in *Murder in the Collective.* Most of the heroes of lesbian crime novels live alone, while maintaining close ties to friends. Although her parents are long dead, Pam Nilsen leaves home after coming out, a move that underscores the Bildungsroman structure of *Murder in the Collective*. As the second Nilsen novel, *Sisters of the Road*, begins, Pam has moved into her own apartment. At age thirty, she is on her own for the first time, experimenting with solitude and with sexual relationships. Coming out, then, is a form of growing up, like a movement from adolescence to adulthood, and of starting over in the world. Katherine Forrest's Kate Delafield is mourning the death of her lover of many years as *Amateur City* opens, living alone but wanting less solitariness. None of the lesbian detectives is truly a loner, although Douglas's Caitlin Reece comes very close, nor is any involved in a long-term monogamous relationship, although Dreher's Stoner McTavish embarks on a serious relationship in the first novel featuring her and remains involved with Gwen through the next two novels, *Something Shady* (1986) and *Grey Magic* (1987).

The living arrangements depicted in these novels simultaneously suggest two deeply interelated themes: the social isolation of the lesbian and the need for lesbian community. Zimmerman says that the protagonist of the lesbian novel of development who perceives the freedom and power of coming out "can travel through the patriarchal landscape to the point of exit into lesbian nation" (p. 246), with the "ultimate goal of the feminist lesbian . . . coming out novel . . . the creation of lesbian community, established through shared experience, visions, and stories" (p. 247). This goal is approached along two paths in lesbian crime novels: one the contribution of the novels themselves to a lesbian tradition in fiction and a second the novels' internal insistence on the importance of lesbian community. Several protagonists feel a powerful sense of relief when they connect with other lesbians, at least partly because coming out to other lesbians is joyous rather than traumatic, but even more importantly because they derive support from shared experiences. Forrest's *Murder at the Nightwood Bar* focuses in part on the significant role played by safe gathering places for lesbians, with the women who frequent the Nightwood Bar forming a lesbian community. Wilson in both Pam Nilsen novels portrays Pam as making connections with other lesbians and receiving important support from them, a theme stressed through the characters Beth and Janis in *Sisters of the Road,* while it is Nyla Wade's realization of the possibility of lesbian community that enables her to accept her lesbian identity in *Mrs. Porter's Letter.*

The feminist movement on the whole values female community, mutual support, and collective action for social change, but lesbian feminist crime novels illustrate the special significance of such community for lesbians. If women as a group have been perceived as dangerous, with each woman embodying a potential threat to patriarchal order—a recurring theme not only of male hard-boiled detective fiction, but also of much male-authored canonical literature—then lesbians pose a very particular challenge to that order in their "rejection of a compulsory way of life," to use Rich's words ("Compulsory Heterosexuality," p. 157). Rich persuasively argues that heterosexuality is a political institution that enforces women's subservience to men and men's "right of physical, economical, and emotional access" to women (p. 155). Lesbian existence, as "the rejection of a compulsory way of life" is "a direct or indirect attack on male right of access to women" (p. 157), an attack punished through the ages by outright persecution and by various more subtle forms of silencing.[9] On a superficial level, then, one might see lesbian community as a defense against patriarchal culture's hostility, with the establishment of community a way both of increasing individual safety and of insuring that lesbian existence becomes, and then remains, visible. Lesbian community, however, is depicted in these novels not merely as a reaction, but as an action; that is, the revolutionary potential of lesbian feminist community—that which "is precisely the thing that patriarchy has most to dread" (Rich, "Meaning," p. 226)—is deeply embedded in these novels as both plot and theme. Whereas hard-boiled detective fiction in particular, and conventional crime fiction generally, tends to objectify women as lawless, immoral predators who use their sexuality to destroy men, lesbian feminist crime fiction redefines the threat lesbians, and potentially all women, pose to men, which is actually threefold: (1) the threat of indifference;[10] (2) the threat of changing the relations of the sexes by placing women at the center of concern; and (3) the threat of radically altering social power relations through a moral vision that does not assume the value of hierarchical order and that does consistently value women's relations to other women.

Most of the crimes investigated in lesbian feminist crime fiction are committed by men against women as a way of enforcing women's obedience to patriarchal order, with the detective's investigation of the crime working as an exposure of the underpinnings of that order and her solution a triumph of the revolutionary potentiality of lesbian feminism. Vicki McConnell's two Nyla Wade books focus on the silencing of lesbian voices and the attempted eradication of lesbian existence. In *Mrs Porter's Letter,* Nyla sets out to investigate the origin of some love letters she finds hidden in a desk she buys. At first, Nyla does not realize she is investigating a crime, but McConnell makes clear the moral criminality of the quite-legal activity Nyla eventually discovers: a lesbian's nephew has pushed her into faking her own death. "Playing dead"—leaving her home, friends, and town, and giving up her claim to most of her fortune—is the only way that this woman can live in peace with her lover. Nyla realizes that she has participated in this woman's silencing by assuming that the love letters were between a man and a woman: "It had never occurred to me to see their eloquent exchange as other than heterosexual. I knew in that nearly painful moment what a victim I was of an ordinary and limited perspective. . . . I hoped never again to be so small in my analysis of love" (p. 198). The socially sanctioned silencing of these women represents the general silencing of lesbians that has made it difficult for Nyla to recognize her own lesbian identity and in the novel is set beside the silencing of female witnesses to a pimp's murder of a prostitute some years before. The pimp counted on the women's fear of reprisals—lesbians and prostitutes themselves, they knew the legal system would neither listen to them nor protect them—to keep them quiet, but they finally find a way to break that silence through covert, collective action: printing up fliers with a description of the pimp's crime and a drawing of him, and distributing them all over the country through a network of prostitutes. The pimp is not arrested, but the novel ends with a cop's remark that "whoever he is, wherever he is, he's out of work now" (p. 210). All the women in this novel triumph by working together: Nyla rescues the lesbian lovers' story from obscure silence and helps the prostitutes write and print the fliers, with both activities contributing toward her finding her own voice and identity as a lesbian.[11] At the same time, McConnell points to connections between the lesbian-hating nephew and the murderous pimp; although on different sides of the law, the two men act on exactly the same system of values, which gives them control over women's lives and bodies. Through descriptions of the two men's similar style of dress and shared preference for chauffeured limousines, McConnell suggests that the nephew may well be the pimp, thereby emphasizing how little there is to choose between them.

The second Nyla Wade novel, *The Burnton Widows,* shows Nyla joining with lesbians and gay men to defeat the destruction of a tangible symbol of lesbian existence—a castle built by women and continuously inhabited by lesbians for 125 years—and to expose the murderer of the two lesbians who most recently owned it. To learn about the castle's history and then to investigate the murders, which are officially considered solved, Nyla must first overcome the town's conspiracy of silence: people seem to think that if they just forget the murders and allow the castle to be torn down to make way for a new resort, the lesbian history of the castle will vanish as well. The proponents of the new resort and the actual murderers of the lesbian lovers unsurprisingly turn out to be the same people, a conspiracy of the town's most powerful men. As in *Mrs. Porter's Letter,* though, Nyla prevails, and the castle is preserved through collective action. In both novels, McConnell attaches an almost mystical power to words, with Nyla's success in every case significantly linked to words—the words of Mrs. Porter's letters, of the flier, of the history of the castle, and of the lesbian love poems written by one of the now-dead women and preserved by Nyla—a linkage most appropriate to novels that concern themselves with the importance of lesbians breaking silence.

The threat of indifference that lesbians pose to men and violent, specifically sexual male responses to that threat are components of *Mrs. Porter's Letter, Stoner McTavish, The Always Anonymous Beast,* and *The Monarchs Are Flying.* In each of these four novels, one man is shown to be enraged by lesbians, taking their existence as a personal challenge to his masculinity and responding to that imagined personal affront with terrifying violence. The politician who murdered the two lesbians in *The Burnton Widows*—a man who has no remorse for his crime, and who worries about his coconspirators in revealing terms: "Too many weaklings, in war and life, only a few good men" (p. 233)—is given a history that includes visiting Japanese brothels to buy displays of pseudo-lesbian sex among groups of women whom he would then sometimes beat up.[12] The murderer in *The Monarchs Are Flying* married a woman because he saw her lesbianism as a challenge; this man then beats his wife when she refuses to live entirely under his rule, and eventually murders her, mutilating her body in a way that makes clear his sexual fury.[13] Another husband, in *The Always Anonymous Beast,* feels so threatened by his wife's lesbian crush that he ends up murdering three of the six people who know about it and trying to murder the other three; he describes his planned murder of his wife as a way of "chastising" her, having got away with "chastising" his first wife thirty years before (p. 202). Gwen's husband in *Stoner McTavish* rapes her to punish her for her (nonsexual as yet) intimacy with Stoner. It is later revealed that he has a history of assault and rape, making a career of punishing women, just as he planned to punish Gwen. He tells Stoner he has "fun" planning to kill Gwen, whom he describes as a "stupid cow," and has considered delaying the murder, "playing with her a little. Just enough to scare her. Just enough to make it interesting" (p. 178). All these men harbor a determination to force women to submit to them—sexually, economically, physically—no matter what the cost, in this way serving as extreme examples of a wish widely shared by men and encoded in the general culture as man's right. Of course, not all men in these novels are murderous, enraged misogynists, but those that are stand not as aberrations but as frighteningly logical extensions of conventionally accepted attitudes, with their violence placed on a continuum of crimes against women that are often not legally defined as crimes at all or, if they are, not treated seriously by the legal system.

Many lesbian feminist crime novels focus on this idea of a

continuum of crimes against women in general and, often, lesbians in particular, locating the ideological basis of those crimes in precisely the same system that claims to protect women: the heterosexist, patriarchal underpinnings of the law, these novels show, actually encourage violence against women. *Sisters of the Road,* for instance, demonstrates the connections among the sexual abuse of children, forced prostitution, rape, and murder by carefully tracing each back to male domination of women and children and the social treatment of females of all ages as sexual objects and as objects of exchange among men. At the beginning of this novel, Pam brings a badly beaten teenage ex-prostitute to the hospital, where the girl dies. Hoping to save the victim's equally young friend from a similar fate, Pam embarks on a search for the living girl, Trish, while also trying to discover who killed Rosalie. Pam learns that Rosalie, a lesbian who wanted to quit prostitution, was murdered by her pimp because she was also trying to get Trish off the streets and, he says, "Trish belongs to *me*" (p. 193). Before this discovery, though, Pam learns that Trish was sexually abused by her father (who attributes this abuse to "the Devil in me"); given up to the state by her stepfather, who beat her because she is "a whore and she's always been a whore" (p. 62), and her mother, whose allegiance to her husband leads her to choose him over her daughter; and set to work as a prostitute at thirteen by her stepbrother Wayne. Ultimately, Pam is raped by that stepbrother, the pimp, who plans also to kill her as "a lesson to Trish" (p. 193); the stream of abuse the rapist unleashes at Pam as he beats and rapes her ("Bitch, cunt, lezzie, pervert, whore, how do you like this, you fucking dyke" [p. 194]) intensifies the horror of the scene while making the motive for the rape—assertion of dominance—terrifyingly clear.[14] The sexual abuse of a female child by her father begins the cycle of violence that culminates in a woman's murder in *Murder at the Nightwood Bar,* with the mother's total investment in denying that abuse ever happened eventually leading her to kill her daughter while trying to silence her.

These brief synopses may make these two novels seem like tracts about male violence against women and women's unending victimization, an impression I want to correct by considering the actual hopefulness of the novels. Like McConnell's Nyla Wade books, *Sisters of the Road* and *Murder at the Nightwood Bar* end optimistically, with Wilson showing Pam saved from murder by her friend June and helping Trish toward a freer future by rescuing her from Wayne, and Forrest including a final scene at a gay-pride parade, where Kate watches a group march proudly under the banner "Parents and Friends of Lesbians and Gays." Similarly, Stoner prevents Brian's murder of Gwen, another lesbian saves Caitlin and herself from murder, Harriet exposes the real killer and vindicates Leslie, and Marjorie steps forward to prevent Nan's self-sacrifice, gaining the support of a large group of women and eventually being acquitted of murder on the grounds of self-defense. These novels' conclusions suggest that lesbians (and straight women) speaking the truth about their lives and acting together in support of each other, collectively and individually, will eventually defeat the patriarchal order and, along the way to that goal, will continue to triumph over threatening manifestations of that order. Crime fiction, then, becomes a vehicle not of reassurance that God is in His heaven and all is right with the world, but of hope that the world can be put right by dismantling exactly the order traditional crime fiction usually seeks to uphold.

The detective's role in lesbian crime novels often bears little resemblance to that of either traditional or heterosexual feminist detectives. The most conventional detective in this group is Kate Delafield, Katherine Forrest's police detective. Kate works for the homicide division of the LAPD, alongside a male partner who admires her but who embodies many attitudes and values she finds repugnant. Like the straight women police officers discussed in chapter 4, Kate is depicted as struggling to reconcile her personal values with the hierarchical, masculinist police department for which she works. She is often reminded that she is nearly anomalous, feeling on these occasions "the familiar heavy weariness at being reminded of her singularity. The tired knowledge that always she was silhouetted against her background" (*Amateur City*, p. 25). Kate sees herself as one of a "thin blue line of men and women who did their best to protect and to serve" but wonders "how much longer [they could] hold back such ferocity" as indicated by the projection she recalls that "soon one out of three American men would have in his past a perpetration of violence" (p. 14). Kate explains her reasons for joining the police force as wanting to "help" people and for staying as a fascination with "the raw edges of lives I could never imagine" (p. 182). Kate never mentions liking the feeling of power, but enjoying some measure of power is evidently another reason she stays with the job. In *Murder at the Nightwood Bar,* she stops several men from kidnapping and raping a woman; a group of lesbians has tried to fight off the men, but the men have beaten them back with lead pipes. Kate is able to succeed here because she is an officer with a gun. Kate becomes enraged when one of the men taunts the women with "make me puke, dykes," and "all control left her" (p. 102). She badly beats this man, breaking his nose. This is a more violent version of Kate Miskin's admission in *A Taste for Death* of feeling "elation" after questioning an arrogant, upper-class man: the pleasure of having power, even if just for a moment, over those who are usually in the powerful position. Accused by other lesbians in *Murder at the Nightwood Bar* of having "sold out to her own oppressors" (p. 15) and working to protect "heterosexual white middle class males and their female slaves" (p. 110), Kate believes there is a "kernel of truth" in the accusations but responds with "All I can do as an individual police officer is try to make the laws of this country apply to everyone. And I think that's worth doing" (p. 110). Perhaps it is true that a police department with lesbian officers is preferable to one without them, but it is also clear that it would take a vast infusion of lesbians to alter police departments significantly. Furthermore, neither in the narrative nor through Kate's speech does Forrest address the larger question: is applying this country's laws to everyone going to solve the widespread social problems these two novels explore (racism, sexism, homophobia, child abuse, wife battering, etc.)? The laws themselves may well be part of those problems, thus enforcing them is hardly a solution. The fairly positive attitude toward the law in Forrest's novels helps to explain Kate's relative conventionality as a detective, which in turn leads to rather conventional plot structures. Forrest in both novels begins with a crime and then follows Kate as she assembles the clues to that crime, with the criminal's arrest concluding both mysteries. Kate never doubts her ability to get to the truth, nor does Forrest deeply question the value of the detective's role.

In contrast, the other lesbian detectives work in less conventional ways, with the novels that focus on them offering varying degrees of challenge to the conventions of crime fiction. Lauren Wright Douglas's Caitlin Reece in some particulars closely resembles other feminist private eyes—she carries a gun, uses illegal methods to solve cases, enjoys the independence she gains through self-employment, gets sexually and emotionally involved with a person who figures in her current case, traces her choice of career to disillusionment working within the legal system—but her two differences, apart from her lesbianism, overshadow the similarities: she takes only cases to which she is morally committed, in which she can act to help those the system cannot or will not help, and she is psychic. Caitlin wants to see herself as an "analytical sleuth, solving the riddle by the cold clear light of logic" (p. 193); therefore she tries to ignore her intuitions, but she also acknowledges that her clairvoyance can be helpful, especially if she rules it instead of letting it rule her as it has ruled other women in her family. McConnell and Dreher also use varieties of supernaturalism in their novels. In *Stoner McTavish*, Stoner's fortune-teller aunt warns her of what will happen, and Stoner uses this knowledge to prevent a crime instead of waiting to uncover the solution to one; in *Gray Magic* Dreher uses Hopi mysticism as the center of her plot, with Stoner actually battling spirits.[15] McConnell has Nyla repeatedly experience the same vision in *Mrs. Porter's Letter*: a large scarlet flower "closing and opening, in and out like film slowed down and then speeded up" (p. 20). Nyla's friend Audrey Louise points out the obvious sexual imagery and suggests the flower "is some kind of weird clue" to the letters (p. 43), as indeed it is: had Nyla linked the vision and the letters earlier, she might at least have thought of the possibility that the letters are lesbian love letters. These novels challenge the usual privileging of logic and reason over intuition and emotion in crime fiction, while suggesting that there are different ways of knowing and that no single method is adequate alone or intrinsically better than any other. Valerie Miner's Nan Weaver and

Marion Foster's two main characters are certainly not detectives.[16] Nan knows Marjorie committed the murder, and the novel traces Nan's attempts to *hide* this knowledge from, not expose it to, others, even after she is put on trial for the murder herself; the real crime in *Murder in the English Department* is not the murder but the rape that preceded it and the real puzzle is not who did it, which is never in doubt, but Marjorie's prolonged refusal of connections with other women. Harriet does uncover the real murderer, but her interest is less in who did it and why than in showing that Leslie did *not* do it.

Only Barbara Wilson's Pam Nilsen among the lesbian detectives devotes herself to solving crimes, yet *Murder in the Collective* and *Sisters of the Road* also present the most radical revisions of the detective's role, not only in their challenge to ideas of order (the crimes Pam investigates are *part* of the social order, not violations of it) but also in their antiauthoritarian stance. Pam does solve the mysteries with which she is presented, but the value of that activity is called into question. The most powerful voice in the final chapters of *Murder in the Collective* is one that disputes the validity of the detective's role. Pam is about to unmask the murderer, opening her unraveling of the crime with a statement that echoes other detectives ("There's only one person who links the two events together, only one person who was at both places, only one person who is the obvious suspect" [p. 174], when another woman begins to challenge her. This woman mocks Pam's assurance and then says, "You go around acting like detectives, you and that Hadley girl, pointing your finger here and there and here again. You maybe hide Zee but you give her up without a word when the time comes. You say, we're going to find out the truth, and you, June, get your ass to California. We don't need you around making any complications. You go around and then you settle back on Zee with any speck of proof" (p. 175). After this challenge, Pam finally begins to question just what it is she thinks she's doing and just what the result of her investigation might be: another woman's incarceration. She feels "at a loss":

I suddenly wondered why it was all so important. What did it matter if Zee had done it, or June had, as she claimed? Jeremy had been a dangerous person, missed by no one except his family who remembered him the way he used to be at seven or eight, blond, sweet, sitting on a hired horse. (pp. 175–76)

She comes to realize that she has been behaving foolishly, and in a way that might damage another woman. After the truth comes out—that Zee did indeed kill Jeremy, to prevent his blackmailing a lesbian for money and sex—Pam acknowledges that June's was the better part: June "hadn't pursued Zee like a detective, she'd confronted her like a woman and stayed to comfort her like a friend" (p. 179). Pam and Hadley regret knowing the truth because now Zee will be "trusting a few too many people with [her] secret" (p. 179), but they decide to help Zee hide that secret from the police. The novel suggests that Pam's discovery of the facts is far less important than her discovery that women, collectively and individually, are more valuable than abstract ideas of justice, and far more worth protecting. In other words, she learns from June's response to Zee and Zee's own explanation of the murder the lesson Zee had tried to teach her earlier: "You [have] to understand about women in the other parts of the world and . . . learn to care about them to be a feminist" (p. 179). This novel is left open-ended in some ways—no one knows for certain what happens to Zee, for instance, or if the other women's decision to keep her secret helps her elude the police—but the crucial changes in Pam carry over into *Sisters of the Road,* where we find her trying to act on that concern for other women. She searches for Rosalie's killer not because she thinks finding him and having him punished will serve justice, but because she cares about Trish and wants to protect her. These two novels strongly imply that feminists, straight and lesbian, owe other women concern and care, and that feminist morality must put women, and relations among women, at its center.

Wilson connects lesbian feminism to other social issues through Pam's discoveries about Jeremy and her conversations with other women in *Murder in the Collective* in a strategy characteristic of lesbian feminist crime novels. Much as these novels tend to depict crimes as part of a larger social pattern, so too do they refuse to treat lesbian identity in isolation. Although other feminist crime novels often incorporate a variety of social issues,[17] lesbian crime novels tend to do so more consistently and in a more unified political fashion. This concern with the intersections of various kinds of oppression—race, class, sex, sexuality—may be the result of the social outsider's ability to see society's flaws more clearly than can those who enjoy that society's privileges, a possibility also reflected in the numerous social analyses lesbian feminists have been publishing and discussing in recent years.[18] June, a black character in *Collective*, voices an awareness of the lesbian's special sensitivity to varieties of oppression when she tells Pam that "you are so liberal you don't even know how liberal you are. . . . Though now you're a lesbian there may be some hope for you" (p. 176). *Collective's* murder victim is an informer and blackmailer who has infiltrated anti-Marcos groups; Zee, who is an anti-Marcos activist, describes to Pam the Marcos regime's violent suppression of opposition and the US's encouragement of Third World women's prostitution.[19] June and Zee together prompt Pam to examine and to work against her own racism.

Miner treats class biases and sexual harassment in *Murder in the English Department*, with both problems portrayed as deeply entrenched in society and therefore resistant to initiatives for change. Nan Weaver heads the university's Sexual Harassment Campaign; because this work is a profound challenge to the existing power structure, Nan risks tenure denial by engaging in it. Several people warn her to lie low until she is granted tenure and she meets resistance even from some women she hopes to help, including Marjorie, Nan's advisee who asks Nan if one "could get a little, um, hysterical about these things?" (p. 19). Marjorie's remark proves deeply ironic, as she becomes the victim of an attempted rape by the English Department's most notorious sexual harasser, whom she kills while fighting off his attack. Nan cannot put her commitment to this campaign or to women generally in abeyance just because it would be more politic to do so if she wants tenure, any more than she can suddenly stop being a middle-class woman of Catholic, working-class origins. The subtleties of class biases and the impact of class on each person's life are brilliantly handled by Miner, who shows Nan as set apart in academe by her working-class background but also set apart from

her family by her middle-class education and the political attitudes it has engendered. Miner shows that class bias cuts all ways,
with misunderstandings and outright hostility springing from
class assumptions. Nan also feels some distance from the upper-
class Marjorie, whose monied, privileged background has given
her self-assurance; Nan "knew that a lot of rich people were im-
pervious to danger. It was as if they never learned a whole set of
survival signals" (p. 72). The novel insists that it is difficult, but
possible, to bridge the divide of class, with Nan feeling close both
to her sister and to Marjorie's mother and Marjorie and Nan's
niece becoming friends. Miner suggests that the things that link
women—symbolized here by sexual harassment and by Nan's defense of Marjorie—are more powerful than the things that divide
them, such as class.

McConnell, Forrest, and Wilson treat prostitution as a feminist
issue, with Wilson's *Sisters of the Road* offering the most complex
analysis. Pam Nilsen's moderate feminist anti-prostitution stance is
challenged when she meets a prostitute who conforms to none of
the common stereotypes. A lesbian lawyer helping Pam search for
Trish takes Pam to task for assuming all prostitutes are only or
simply victims of male oppression, saying, "Who am I—or any
feminist—to decide whether prostitution is a good or bad thing
for the women who do it? . . . Most prostitutes I've met feel like
they're the ones in control, using men to get back what's owing to
them economically" (p. 128). Pam and this woman argue back and
forth, with Pam pointing out that not all prostitutes have a choice
("A lot of them are young girls who've been victims of sexual
abuse and they go on being victimized" [p. 131]) and Janis countering with "Even victims have a choice. . . . Survival is a choice
and prostitution is a means of economic survival" (p. 132). Dawn,
the prostitute Pam meets through Janis, says that prostitutes are
"not monsters, we're not all on heroin and we do lead happy,
fulfilled lives, at least about as often as so-called regular people
do" (p. 144) and wonders "why feminists think they're so much
better than we are, why they can't see this from our point of view"
(p. 147). This discussion, and the rest of the novel, eloquently
demonstrates the point that feminists, both straight and lesbian,
do indeed have much in common with prostitutes: not all are

simply victims, all make choices among variously limited possibilities, all face the potential of male violence, and all can benefit from alliances with others. Neither Pam nor Janis "wins" the debate about prostitution; instead, each moves a bit closer toward understanding the other's position, with Pam acknowledging the persuasiveness of Dawn's personal experience and Janis acknowledging the dangers of working as a prostitute. This admission of multiple points of view, without a hierarchical ordering of them or any attempt to persuade the reader to choose one position over another, is characteristic of feminist crime novels and especially of lesbian feminist ones, which enact in their narrative structures a commitment to mutual respect and egalitarianism. *Sisters of the Road's* treatment of prostitution is an especially interesting example of this tolerance of diversity, but it is also evident in other novels, such as in the discussions of nonviolence in *The Always Anonymous Beast.* Caitlin insists at first that violence is the only effective response to violence, whereas Tonia Konig, a professor of women's studies, is totally committed to the principle of nonviolence, but each learns that the other's point of view merits consideration, Caitlin when she hears Tonia's classroom lecture on nonviolence as a form of action and Tonia when she can save Caitlin from death only by taking violent action. The reader is left to make one choice or the other, with no choice excluded from the narrative.

The issue of women and violence comes up in most lesbian crime novels. As mentioned earlier, Forrest shows Kate Delafield enjoying her own violent response to male, anti-lesbian violence in a scene that demonstrates that nonviolent action against some aggressors would be useless. Douglas's Caitlin, who (illegally) carries a concealed gun, tells Tonia she does not enjoy hurting others, but admits to the reader that this is a lie: "Sometimes, I *did* enjoy the scaring, breaking, and shooting. Sometimes, seeing a look of abject terror come into some pimple-faced punk's eyes, and knowing it was I, not he who had power—and that *he knew it*—was enjoyable in itself. And it scared the hell out of me" (p. 31). This sounds very much like the scene in Paretsky's *Killing Orders,* described in chapter 5, where V. I. is simultaneously disturbed by her own violent behavior toward a thug and pleased that she has the power in this situation. Recognizing her own violent impulses and occasional enjoyment of acting out these impulses seems to call into question some important part of the woman detective's self-concept, partly because of women's socialization into nurturing roles, I think, but also because violent propensities suggest the detective is in some sense implicated in the very structure of power she understands to be corrupt and deeply opposed to life. Again, it is Wilson who highlights the ambiguities of this issue. In *Sisters of the Road*, Pam watches an episode of *Cagney and Lacey* in which a young woman officer ambushes and kills a rapist, taking "the law into her own hands because the law didn't protect women" (pp. 160–61). The television program ends without offering comment on the woman's action:

> And I almost burst into tears. It was as if I understood the story on some profound level and was afraid of its meaning. Was that the only way to stop violence against women? To kill men? To kill them back?
> I didn't want to believe that. (p. 161)

Later, when Wayne is raping Pam, June bursts into the cabin and begins beating the rapist with a ski pole. Pam says that if the state police officers "right behind her, hadn't stopped her, she would have killed him. I'm sure of that" (p. 194). June does not kill Wayne, but it is clear that only deadly force would stop him, as it is the possibility of being killed by the police that ends his rape of Pam. Wilson never directly endorses violence, yet the novel does suggest that, regardless of what one wants to believe, violence may sometimes be the only option that does not require one's own death.

Not all lesbian crime novels demonstrate the tolerance for diversity or for ambiguity seen in Wilson, though, and several do slide into an unfortunate didacticism. In *The Monarchs Are Flying*, for example, Foster includes several pages of supposed courtroom testimony that amounts to a lecture on the normality of lesbian and gay lives, in which a psychologist well versed in recent psychological literature demolishes the antiquated, anti-gay views of a psychiatrist who views homosexuality as a failure to adapt to society. The space devoted to this section and Foster's portrayal of the testimony as crucial, intended to convert possibly heterosexist members of the jury, raise questions about the audience Foster is trying to reach: suddenly the novel seems less a novel than it does well-intentioned propaganda aimed at straight, homophobic readers or at lesbians who have not yet accepted a lesbian identity. No one likes to be lectured, especially in such obvious terms; this section therefore seems a poor choice by Foster, with the problem exacerbated by the section's coming toward the end of the book, which never has a chance to recover from it. Furthermore, I question Foster's decision to give the voice of authority to a straight, white, male character, as this choice undercuts the novel's theme of women, especially lesbians, needing to reject patriarchal definitions in order to develop self-definitions. Allowing a male character to define *lesbian* is giving up the right of naming to another who does not, and cannot, live the experience he names and implicitly assenting to only slight modifications in the existing power structure.

Foster's reliance on external authorities is unusual in lesbian crime novels, which tend in fact to position themselves against the whole notion of authority. Because these novels join at least three traditions—the crime novel, the lesbian novel of development, and the feminist novel—they often offer more direct critiques of genre conventions than do other feminist crime novels, radically revising, as has been seen, the detective's role, the issue of social order, and the conception of crime as a violation of order. Several lesbian feminist crime novels make explicit, and therefore inescapable, the ideological conflicts between feminism and particular subgenres of crime novels that are more covertly treated in most of the novels discussed in the preceding four chapters. Katherine V. Forrest, despite choosing not to pursue some larger questions about the underlying assumptions governing the institution of the police, nevertheless does examine the internal conflicts a woman police officer might experience much more intensely than do most other female authors of police procedurals, with the procedure itself also portrayed as problematic. Kate Delafield's doubled outsider status—as woman and as lesbian—allows her special sensitivity to the entrenched masculinist biases of the police. These masculinist biases, including an insistence on valuing "facts" over intuitions, work against the police's attempts to solve the crime in *Murder at the Nightwood Bar*, where it is Kate's lesbianism and feminism that enable her to reach a solution. Furthermore, unlike the authors of most police procedurals, Forrest does not assume readers' interest in police routine; instead, she assumes interest in the details of lesbian existence.

Valerie Miner's *Murder in the English Department* goes even further, with solving a crime essentially a nonissue and the appropriate response to that crime infinitely more important. If this novel is put beside other feminist crime novels set in academe, Miner's break with convention becomes even more startling. Amanda Cross's last three novels raise questions about the idea of the university, especially the prestigious university, but offer the optimistic hope that such universities are capable of change and will indeed change as increasing numbers of feminist women work from within for change. Through Nan Weaver, Miner examines the attraction of the university for a working-class woman, acknowledging the possibilities for escape from narrow, class- and gender-limited lives the university seems to offer, but also considers the barriers academe presents to women. Nan's absolute commitment to the Sexual Harassment Campaign implies optimism akin to Amanda Cross's, but the novel's conclusion suggests that the tremendous work required to make even small changes in academe may be a misuse of women's energy and passion. As the novel ends, Nan is considering leaving Berkeley but continuing to teach. She thinks that perhaps places with less prestige will have less sexism as well and will not "fear and despise" her for her feminism (p. 167). Whether this is an accurate analysis of the comparative misogyny of more or less prestigious universities is open to debate, as Nan tells herself, but the sense of freedom Miner depicts in Nan after she realizes her options are open—she rides off to the mountains, singing along to her car radio—indicates that Miner thinks that choosing to leave might make sense. The reader is likely to agree, as this novel's portrayal of sexual harassment and the university's inadequate response to that harassment together suggest that prestigious universities may well be irredeemable, with women's energy and time best used somewhere else.

The deepest questioning of genre conventions occurs in Barbara Wilson's *Murder in the Collective*, where the activities of an amateur detective are shown to be in possible opposition to women's interests, as discussed earlier. The question Wilson has Pam ask herself—"why it was all so important" (p. 175)—becomes also a question for the reader, inviting consideration of why feminists read crime fiction at all. Pam's other important question is "What did we ever really solve?" (p. 180), which calls attention to the larger social problems of which the crimes investigated in lesbian novels are microcosmic manifestations. This is the question that, although seldom so directly stated, haunts the final pages of *all* feminist crime novels.

7

Conclusion

In a chapter of *Villette* (1853) ironically titled "Fraternity," Charlotte Brontë's narrator-protagonist is interrogated by two male professors who believe another man has forged Lucy's name to an essay he wrote. Convinced that no woman could write so well, the professors insist that Lucy prove her authorship by composing an essay on "Human Justice" as they watch. Suddenly recognizing the professors as the men who harassed her in the street one night, Lucy finds inspiration in rage:

"Human Justice" rushed before me in novel guise, a red, random beldame with arms akimbo. I saw her in her house, the den of confusion: servants called to her for orders or help which she did not give; beggars stood at her door waiting and starving unnoticed; a swarm of children, sick and quarrelsome, crawled round her feet and yelled in her ears appeals for notice, sympathy, cure, redress. The honest woman cared for none of these things. She had a warm seat of her own by the fire, she had her own solace in a short black pipe, and a bottle of Mrs. Sweeny's soothing syrup; she smoked and she sipped and she enjoyed her paradise, and whenever a cry of the suffering souls about her pierced her ears too keenly—my jolly dame seized the poker or the hearth-brush; if the offender was weak, wronged, and sickly, she effectually settled him; if he was strong, lively, and violent, she only menaced, then plunged her hand in her deep pouch, and flung a liberal shower of sugar-plums. (p. 386)

Although they probably would not personify justice as female, many of the writers discussed in the preceding six chapters could use Brontë's angry description of "human justice" as their novels' epigraph. As has been noted, feminist crime novels often show social order to be actually a "den of confusion," wherein the powerless are "effectually settled" while the powerful enjoy "a liberal shower of sugar-plums." Only shifting the balance of power will put human justice's house in order and allow "appeals for notice, sympathy, cure, redress" to be heard.

I want to return for a moment to my assertion in the first chapter that women writers are creating a countertradition in crime fiction, with this countertradition the most recent flowering of a female literary tradition at least two centuries old. The images of enclosure and entrapment in Liza Cody's *Bad Company,* for instance, rework the imprisonment theme of Radcliffe's *The Mysteries of Udolpho,* but with a crucial difference in the female hero's attitude and ability to fight back, while P. D. James's *A Taste of Death* and Barbara Wilson's *Sisters of the Road,* to mention but two of many, echo the theme of domestic, familial horror that informs Mary Shelley's *Frankenstein.* Most striking are the parallels between nineteenth-century sensation fiction and contemporary feminist crime novels. Women sensation novelists "invert[ed] the stereotypes of the domestic novel and parod[ied] the conventions of their male contemporaries" (Showalter, *Literature,* p. 160), demanding sympathy for their criminal heroines (Hughes, p. 108), whose sins are shown to result from patriarchal imperatives. Feminist crime writers, like sensation novelists before them, frequently locate the source of crime in attitudes that underpin the patriarchy, with their female murderers generally male-identified women acting in desperation, like Marian Harwood in *The Down East Murders,* Connie Byrnes in *A Little Madness,* and Dory Quillen's mother in *Murder at the Nightwood Bar.* Elaine Showalter's point that sensation novelists depict as most dangerous the " 'pretty little girl' whose indoctrination in the female role has taught her secrecy and deceitfulness, almost as secondary sex characteristics" (*Literature,* p. 165) applies equally aptly to those feminist crime novels with female villains, such as Marcia Muller's *The Tree of Death* and Sara Paretsky's *Killing Orders.* Looked at from this perspective, even those few women, like Lillian O'Donnell, who seem to follow male crime writers in depicting women as the source of crime and, as I argued in chapter 4, endorse stereotypical views of women, could be read like sensation novelists, with their work then seen not necessarily as illustrative of male fears but of female fantasies. Like gothic and sensation novels, feminist crime fiction displaces the traditionally central male consciousness, offering instead a woman-centered world view.

Sensation fiction arose at a time when women were attempting to destroy the male publishing monopoly, founding presses and feminist journals, editing magazines, and reviewing manuscripts for mainstream publishers (Showalter, *Literature*, pp. 154–57). Feminist crime fiction is emerging at a similar time in history, as the past twenty years has seen the rise of numerous feminist journals, newspapers, and presses, the publication of important works of feminist scholarship, and the growing influence of feminist thought on culture and society. Blending the themes of gothic and sensation fiction with the methods of detective fiction, feminist writers have created female heroes who challenge received wisdom about women's role and novels that subvert genre conventions. Feminist crime novels, far from being mere escapist literature or isolated, peculiar experiments in an essentially masculine preserve, participate in the larger feminist project of redefining and redistributing power, joining a long and valuable tradition of women's fiction.

Notes

Chapter 1. A Sisterhood of Detection

1. I am using Mikhail Bakhtin's terms—*monologic* and *dialogic*—from *The Dialogic Imagination* fairly loosely, extrapolating from his idea of language as an area of ideological struggle, with *monologic* indicating a text that works like an epic, with a single vision and voice prevailing, and *dialogic* indicating a text in which a variety of ideas and voices speak.

2. Throughout this section I am indebted to Julian Symons's idiosyncratic, invaluable *Bloody Murder*.

3. Anyone who doubts this need only glance through the index of any critical book on detective fiction or read the tables of contents of a few issues of one of the journals dedicated to the genre, such as *Clues* or *The Armchair Detective*.

4. For an entertaining and convincing overview of the damage done women writers' reputations by biased criticism, see Joanna Russ's witty *How to Suppress Women's Writing*.

5. See, for instance, Elaine Showalter's *A Literature of their Own* and Dale Spender's *Mothers of the Novel*.

6. Walter Allen, *The English Novel,* quoted in Spender (p. 241).

7. The eleven essays included in *What Is Feminism?*, edited by Juliet Mitchell and Ann Oakley, both individually and collectively explore the diversity of contemporary feminism. Rosalind Delmar's contribution, also titled "What is Feminism?", provides an excellent historical overview of the evolution of feminism, with Delmar taking the position that "it now makes more sense to speak of a plurality of feminisms than of one" (p. 9). See also Hester Eisenstein's *Contemporary Feminist Thought,* a history and analysis of the development of feminist theory and ideology in the United States.

8. Judith Fetterly, in the introduction to her study of American literature, *The Resisting Reader,* describes the process of learning to read as a man as an important part of "the immasculation of women by men," p. xx. The first book to explore in detail what it means to read as a woman is the volume of essays edited by Patrocinio Schweickart and Elizabeth Flynn, *Gender and Reading*.

9. Women in academe continue to grapple with the masculine norms of the profession; previously barred altogether from the academy, women are now admitted but tend to be denied authority, power, and advancement. See Nadya Aisenberg and Mona Harrington, *Women of Academe: Outsiders in the Sacred Grove.*

Chapter 2. Free-lancing Amateurs

1. Adrienne Rich's analysis of the political function of the public/ private division in "Husband-Right and Father-Right," from which the quote is taken (p. 215), is trenchant. Also helpful is Deborah Gorham's discussion of the Victorian origins of the idea of separate spheres in *The Victorian Girl and the Feminine Ideal*, pp. 3–8.

2. Marty S. Knepper advances this argument in "Agatha Christie— Feminist."

3. The Detection Club's interdiction of romance is one of many strictures it advocated. See Symons, *Bloody Murder*, pp. 13–14, and Ronald Knox, "A Detective Story Decalogue."

4. Dorothy Sayers has Harriet explain her code of ethics in chapter 4 of *Strong Poison.*

5. Although Sarah Deane is in some broad sense an academic, Borthwick's novels are considered here instead of in chapter 3 because academe is not really an issue in them. Borthwick seems to have chosen Sarah's work—graduate student and English teacher—mainly to explain her penchant for literary allusions and her comparative poverty.

6. That female novels of development often describe growing up for women as a process of growing down, as recognizing and accommodating oneself to strict social limitations, is discussed by Annis Pratt in *Archetypal Patterns in Women's Fiction*, (pp. 13–37) and by Elizabeth Abel, Marianne Hirsch, and Elizabeth Langland in their introduction to *The Voyage In: Fiction of Female Development*, pp. 3–19.

7. Some examples include Alice Walker's *Meridian* and *The Color Purple*, Marge Piercy's *Small Changes*, Margaret Atwood's *The Edible Woman*, and Rita Mae Brown's *Rubyfruit Jungle.*

8. Sarah sees Connie Goldsmith as a mother figure. Just after the mirror episode, Connie comes to Sarah's room to see if the younger woman is all right, and "Sarah looked up as if seeing her companion for the first time. I wanted to go home, she thought, and here's a mother ready-made" (p. 77).

9. Pederson-Krag's essay is reprinted in *The Poetics of Murder*, along with other psychoanalytic analyses, such as Jacques Lacan's "Seminar on *The Purloined Letter.*"

10. Judith Kegan Gardiner's examination of the implications of Nancy Chodorow's construction of female psychology for women's writing in "On Female Identity and Writing by Women" argues that the woman writer's relationship with her characters is fluid, with the female hero

often acting as her author's daughter. This section of the chapter springs in part from my application of Gardiner's thesis to Borthwick's *The Down East Murders*.

11. In the most obvious version of this threat, Sidney (the father) attempts to murder Sarah when she finds Elspeth's (the mother's) painting.

12. Several of the characters speak of Marian as "far gone," for instance, or say she "went off" or "snapped."

13. Paul has published three Geraldine Ferrar books thus far: *A Cadenza for Caruso*, *Prima Donna at Large*, and *A Chorus of Detectives*.

14. Anne Morice's Tessa Crichton series includes about a dozen books, with several of the most interesting being *Murder in Outline*, *Murder Post-dated*, and *Death in the Round*.

15. See Chodorow, *The Reproduction of Mothering*, pp. 166–70, for a summary of gender-specific character traits.

16. I have omitted *Beyond the Grave* from this discussion of Muller's Elena Oliverez series because the detective's character is not further developed in this novel, whose major interest is as a curiosity, with Pronzini's nineteenth-century detective, Quincannon, and Muller's Oliverez brought together through a century-old unsolved case. This novel's plotting is extremely awkward; for instance, the movement between the two narratives is badly handled, with Elena discovering not just once but several times that further sections of the Quincannon manuscript are missing and then having to go in search of them. There are two points of interest, though: Elena's Anglo boyfriend breaks off their relationship, saying it obviously just is not working out although Elena thinks it is, and Elena's mother falls ill, thereby forcing Elena to be a source of strength instead of a seeker of strength and nurturance.

17. Dunlap's other series, which features Berkeley police officer Jill Smith, is discussed in chapter 4.

18. Toni Morrison's *Sula* incorporates this theme, to offer just one example.

19. Sara Ruddick's "Maternal Thinking" and Adrienne Rich's *Of Woman Born* both consider this problem in considerable depth.

20. The title of Sandra Gilbert and Susan Gubar's book on nineteenth-century women writers, *The Madwoman in the Attic*, draws attention to this pervasive theme; perhaps the most compelling American use of the imprisoned woman is Charlotte Perkins Gilman's "The Yellow Wall-Paper."

Chapter 3. Death and the Academy

1. As its title suggests, Valerie Miner's *Murder in the English Department* fits this pattern; however, I discuss it in chapter 6, "Lesbian Detectives," because of its inclusion of the female hero's thoughts about "coming out." Miner's novel incorporates a far more radical critique of academe than do

any of the Cross novels, with the protagonist ultimately thinking of leaving UC-Berkeley, an institution much like Kate Fansler's thinly disguised version of Columbia.

2. A recent novel by Elizabeth Atwood Taylor, *Murder at Vassar,* fits neatly with Silver's series, but in title only. The murder in the Taylor novel takes place at Vassar but is not really of Vassar: although the victim is a Vassar alumna killed while attending her sixty-fifth reunion and the detective who investigates the case, also a Vassar alum, takes refuge from a mad scientist type in the Vassar president's house, Vassar serves only as a backdrop for the novel's events.

3. Immediately after the line quoted from "Compulsory Heterosexuality and Lesbian Existence," Rich argues that the idea of a lesbian continuum, if expanded "to embrace many more forms of primary intimacy between and among women, including the sharing of a rich inner life, the bonding against male tyranny, the giving and receiving of practical and political support," can help us "begin to grasp the breadths of female history and psychology" obscured because of narrow, "clinical" definitions of lesbianism, pp. 156–57.

4. Rich suggests that this failure to analyze "whether the search for love and tenderness in both sexes does not originally lead toward women" and the "societal forces which wrench women's emotional and erotic energies away from themselves and other women" is widespread among feminist scholars and theorists, p. 145; I would argue that feminist fiction writers often share in that failure, and that their work, like Silver's, may suffer as a result.

5. Sayers's concern with work is discussed by Kathleen Gregory Klein in "Dorothy Sayers," pp. 29–32.

6. Jeanne Addison Roberts, "Feminist Murder: Amanda Cross Reinvents Womanhood," focuses on the first two chapters of *Reinventing Womanhood,* wherein Heilbrun gives an autobiographical sketch (Roberts, p. 8). I am indebted to Roberts's article throughout this section, as she notices many of the problems in the Cross novels that I discuss here.

7. The words are Heilbrun's, from *Reinventing Womanhood,* p. 31.

8. In *Reinventing Womanhood,* Heilbrun states this idea directly: "I had been born a feminist and never wavered from that position. I do not mean, of course, that I expressed feminist views in the dreary masculinist years after World War II. But I never denied the pain to myself, nor lied about my anger" (p. 16).

9. Heilbrun draws from Hennig's doctoral thesis, "Career Development for Women Executives," later partly reworked in *The Managerial Woman.* See Heilbrun's note 15, p. 215.

10. *Poetic Justice,* for instance, considers student protests of the late 1960s, while *The Question of Max* incorporates a critique of the climate that fostered Watergate.

11. See the section quoted earlier in this chapter, for example, pp. 51–53.

12. This was written and in page proof before Sara Ruddick gave me Joan Smith's *A Masculine Ending,* the first novel in a projected series featuring Loretta Lawson, a British feminist scholar and professor of English literature. If the rest of the series lives up to this novel's promise, it will be very exciting. Lawson investigates a murder she is not sure even happened, while also engaging in a heated debate among members of a feminist publishing collective about masculine endings in French. The novel brings issues in French and Anglo-American feminist literary scholarship to a wider audience, integrating these issues into an ingenious murder mystery whose solution hinges on the problem of sexual identity.

13. The only time Kate Fansler is seen in a classroom is a scene in *The Theban Mysteries,* where she leads a seminar on *Antigone.*

Chapter 4. New Procedures for Police?

1. In *Powers of the Weak,* Elizabeth Janeway analyzes the various strategies members of oppressed groups employ, focusing in particular on women. Accepting the powerful group's definitions and behaving as a token stand in the way of taking collective, more useful action, pp. 235–40.

2. Much of Barbara Lawrence's "Female Detectives: The Feminist—Anti-Feminist Debate" analyzes such stories, including those written by men but featuring women detectives.

3. Dunlap is also the author of the Vejay Haskell series, discussed in chapter 2.

4. Others in this group include Marie Castoire's Vicki Curran novels, such as *The Gold Shield* and *Not One of the Boys;* Lesley Egan's *The Choice of Crimes;* and Dorothy Uhnak's various novels, including *Victims.*

Chapter 5. Loners and Hard-boiled Women

1. French feminists have been most concerned with women's language; in "Writing the Body: Toward an Understanding of l'Écriture Feminine," Ann Rosalind Jones provides an excellent overview of the French feminists' work.

2. This scene in *Killing Orders,* discussed later in the chapter in a different context, ends the novel with Lotty reinterpreting V. I.'s name for her. V. I. has dreamed about the curse of her middle name—Iphigenia—with her mother performing the sacrifice. Lotty points out that the name need not connote the daughter's sacrifice: "For don't you know that in Greek legend Iphigenia is also Artemis the huntress?" p. 277. Lotty's reinterpretation of the name is an act of practical feminist criticism.

3. In "Dashiell Hammett," Steven Marcus says that "being a detective is the realization of an identity, for there are components in it which are beyond or beneath society—and cannot be touched by it—and beyond and beneath reason," p. 207.

4. The first meaning of *millstone*, of course, is "one of a pair of cylindrical stones used in a mill for grinding grain." There may be a joke here as well, for Kinsey is definitely not "one of a pair."

5. Women private detectives also dream a lot, with the dreams reported in great detail and sometimes suggesting the importance of intuitive or extrarational investigative methods. Anna Lee in *Bad Company* and V. I. Warshawski in *Bitter Medicine* have strikingly similar dreams about babies that recall Jane Eyre's famous baby dream.

6. The significance of this tiredness differs, though, as it parallels postcoital exhaustion for the male detectives, which seems not to be the case in the women's novels, since the women writers do not connect their detectives' work to sex and sexuality in quite the same way as the men do.

7. Barbara Lawrence, in "Female Detectives: the Feminist—Anti-Feminist Debate," also notes Marlowe's and other hard-boiled detectives' misogyny, pp. 38–41.

8. *Ms.* magazine named Paretsky one of its 1987 women of the year for her feminist writing and feminist activism, which is detailed in Laura Shapiro's article on Paretsky in the January 1988 issue, pp. 67ff.

9. The "seemed" in this sentence is very important. Nina Baym's *Woman's Fiction* and Judith Fetterly's *The Resisting Reader* are two of several recent feminist studies to consider the wealth of women's writing this construction of the canon purposefully excluded.

10. Lawrence's descriptions of these female detectives are devastatingly, hilariously accurate, pp. 44–45.

11. Quest tales are an intensely masculine genre, with their outer-directed searches and emphases on physical prowess and conquest of others.

12. He is linked to this tradition in other ways as well, of course, including his physical abilities, self-control, and supreme self-confidence.

13. See note 1, chapter 2, on the public/private gender division.

14. Chodorow, *The Reproduction of Mothering: Psychoanalysis and the Sociology of Gender;* Dinnerstein, *The Mermaid and the Minotaur: Sexual Arrangements and Human Malaise;* and Rich, *Of Woman Born: Motherhood as Experience and Institution.*

15. See Adrienne Rich, "Compulsory Heterosexuality and Lesbian Existence," pp. 156–58.

16. Muller invents such relationships also in her Elena Oliverez series, discussed in chapter 2, and in her recent Joanna Stark novel, *The Cavalier in White,* where Joanna spends about half the novel mourning her husband, dead for three years, and the other half beginning a relationship with a man working on the same case she is investigating.

17. This point is hardly a new one, having been made during the "first wave" of feminism in the nineteenth century by many women, including Charlotte Perkins Gilman, and forming a cornerstone of the contemporary feminist movement.

18. Kinsey's living arrangements are typical of the scaled-down lives of these detectives, all of whom live in small places and have few possessions. Only Muller's and Paretsky's heroes actually own property, both buying modest places during the series in which they appear. Both Kinsey and V. I. suffer the loss of even these small places, with V. I.'s apartment burned and Kinsey's converted garage bombed.

19. Cordelia's reflection on animals arises as she thinks about getting back to London, where most of her work involves searching for lost pets: "It was a job that needed doing, one that she was good at. She knew that it couldn't satisfy her forever, but she didn't despise its simplicities; almost she welcomed them. Animals didn't torment themselves with the fear of death, or torment you with the horror of their dying. They didn't burden you with their psychological problems. They didn't worry about their condition. They didn't surround themselves with possessions or live in the past. They didn't scream with pain because of the loss of love. They didn't expect you to lie for them. They didn't try to murder you," *Skull*, p. 327.

20. In *Dupe*, for instance, a police officer picks up the book Anna has been reading, Henry James's *Portrait of a Lady*, and asks, "You're not one of those Women's Libbers, are you?" while "gazing suspiciously at the bent cover" of the novel, p. 173.

21. Anna is run off the road and injured by two police officers in *Stalker* as a warning to get off a case.

Chapter 6. Lesbian Detectives

1. Some of these differences are suggested by Jean E. Kennard in "Ourself Behind Ourself: A Theory for Lesbian Readers" and by Bonnie K. Zimmerman in "What Has Never Been: An Overview of Lesbian Feminist Criticism."

2. Zimmerman defines heterosexism as "the set of values and structures that assumes heterosexuality to be the only natural form of sexual and emotional expression," "What Has," p. 201.

3. There are some parallels with men's attempts at feminist criticism. See Elaine Showalter's "Critical Cross-Dressing: Male Feminists and the Woman of the Year."

4. For other views in the debate over the definition of *lesbianism,* see also Ann Ferguson, Jacquelyn N. Zita, and Kathryn Pyne Addelson's response to Rich, "On 'Compulsory Heterosexuality and Lesbian Existence': Defining the Issues."

5. This pattern is also seen in J. S. Borthwick's Sarah Deane novels, discussed in chapter 2, and in P. D. James's *An Unsuitable Job for a Woman*, discussed in chapter 5.

6. Kennard says that the "theme of discovering 'one's true self' " is frequently employed in lesbian literature, p. 64.

7. These words are very close to Sharon McCone's in *Leave a Message for Willie*, p. 77, quoted in chapter 5, p. 105. Both heterosexual and lesbian writers show women to be dissatisfied with current relations between the sexes, but the heterosexual writers never call heterosexuality itself into question.

8. The tone of Stoner's fantasies and thoughts about Gwen in *Stoner McTavish* is often adolescent and, for me at least, annoying in much the same way the artificially heightened language of romance novels is off-putting. In fact, the series owes as much to the recent Harlequin romance novel genre as it does to crime fiction, with *Something Shady* listing *Stoner McTavish* as a "Lesbian mystery, romance," A sample from *Stoner McTavish* may illustrate: Gwen casually touches Stoner on the wrist and "the touch traveled up her arm, through her body, and out the soles of her feet. When she got up, she knew, there would be charred spots on the floor" (pp. 83–84). A little of this goes a very long way.

9. Rich lists some of the ways lesbians have been silenced in "The Meaning of Our Love for Women Is What We Have Constantly to Expand," pp. 224–26 and in "Compulsory Heterosexuality and Lesbian Existence," pp. 157–58.

10. In "Compulsory," Rich mentions this threat, saying the male fear of women is "that women could be indifferent to them altogether, that men could be allowed sexual and emotional—therefore economic—access to women *only* on women's terms," p. 151.

11. Given this interest in the lesbian woman's finding her voice, I think it a bit odd that McConnell, whose first novel uses Nyla as the first-person narrator, switches to an omniscient, impersonal narrator in *The Burnton Widows*.

12. This man's behavior seems an acting out of one staple of pornography: the "lesbians" who "perform" for the male's pleasure and who are therefore *not* beyond male control of their sexuality.

13. The woman is beaten with a woman's shoe, all her bodily hair is shaved off, and a towel bar is shoved into her vagina.

14. The scene is horrifying, but far from gratuitous. Wilson evidently wants the reader to confront exactly what rape is, and, through Pam, to imaginatively identify with the victim. Pam feels her whole self is being destroyed: "I felt that whatever made Pam a person, whatever I knew or had known about myself was being crushed out of me, was spinning into fragments like a planet smashed by meteors," p. 194.

15. Readers more interested in mysticism than I am may find this novel more fascinating than I do. I found it actually impossible to read, with the combination of Harlequin-type romance elements and pseudo-Hopi mysticism defeating me about halfway through.

16. Miner did not write *Murder in the English Department* as a mystery, although it is certainly a crime novel. In a highly entertaining talk at the

Modern Language Association convention in December 1984, Miner expressed some surprise at being invited to substitute for a panelist at a session called "Lives in Crime: What Happens When Academics Write Detective Fiction," but went on to point out concerns shared by her book and Cross's *Death in a Tenured Position* (Heilbrun was also on the panel). One could argue that Miner's novel is not crime fiction at all; however, I have included the book here precisely because it directly challenges conventional genre boundaries.

17. Paretsky, for instance, considers health care and anti-abortion activism in *Bitter Medicine;* Muller writes of homelessness and Southeast Asian refugees in *There's Nothing to Be Afraid Of;* and Silver discusses racism in *Death of a Harvard Freshman.*

18. To give just three examples: Andrea Dworkin's *Right Wing Women,* Catharine A. MacKinnon's *Sexual Harassment of Working Women: A Case of Sex Discrimination,* and Mary Daly's *Gyn/Ecology.*

19. The novel is set in 1982, before the ouster of Marcos.

Bibliography

CRIME NOVELS

(The most commonly available editions are listed)

Borthwick, J. S. *The Case of the Hook-Billed Kites*. New York: St. Martins, 1982.

_____. *The Down East Murders*. New York: St. Martin's, 1985.

Cody, Liza. *Bad Company*. 1982. New York: Warner, 1984.

_____. *Dupe*. 1981. New York: Warner, 1983.

_____. *Head Case*. New York: Scribner's, 1985.

_____. *Stalker*. 1984. New York: Warner, 1986.

_____. *Under Contract*. New York: Scribner's, 1986.

Cross, Amanda. *Death in a Tenured Position*. 1981. New York: Ballantine, 1982.

_____. *In the Last Analysis*. 1964. New York: Avon, 1966.

_____. *The James Joyce Murder*. 1967. New York: Ballantine, 1982.

_____. *No Word from Winifred*. New York: Dutton, 1986.

_____. *Poetic Justice*. 1970. New York: Avon, 1972.

_____. *The Question of Max*. 1976. New York: Ballantine, 1984.

_____. *Sweet Death, Kind Death*. 1984. New York: Ballantine, 1985.

_____. *The Theban Mysteries*. 1971. New York: Avon, 1979.

Douglas, Lauren Wright. *The Always Anonymous Beast*. Tallahassee: Naiad, 1987.

Dreher, Sarah. *Gray Magic*. Norwich, VT: New Victoria, 1987.

_____. *Something Shady*. Norwich, VT: New Victoria, 1986.

_____. *Stoner McTavish*. Lebanon, NH: New Victoria, 1985.

Dunlap, Susan. *As a Favor*. New York: St. Martin's, 1984.

_____. *The Bohemian Connection*. New York: St. Martin's, 1985.

_____. *An Equal Opportunity Death*. New York: St. Martin's, 1984.

_____. *The Last Annual Slugfest*. New York: St. Martin's, 1986.

_____. *Not Exactly a Brahmin*. New York: St. Martin's, 1985.

_____. *Too Close to the Edge*. New York: St. Martin's, 1987.

Forrest, Katherine V. *Amateur City*. Tallahassee: Naiad, 1984.

_____. *Murder at the Nightwood Bar*. Tallahassee: Naiad, 1987.

Foster, Marion. *The Monarchs Are Flying*. Ithaca: Firebrand, 1987.

Grafton, Sue. *"A" is for Alibi*. 1982. New York: Bantam, 1987.

_____. *"B" is for Burglar.* 1985. New York: Bantam, 1986.

_____. *"C" is for Corpse.* New York: Henry Holt, 1986.

_____. *"D" is for Deadbeat.* New York: Henry Holt, 1987.

_____. *"E" is for Evidence.* New York: Henry Holt, 1988.

James, P. D. *The Skull Beneath the Skin.* New York: Scribner's, 1982.

_____. *A Taste for Death.* 1986. New York: Warner, 1987.

_____. *An Unsuitable Job for a Woman.* 1972. New York: Warner, 1982.

Kallen, Lucille. *Introducing C. B. Greenfield.* New York: Ballantine, 1981.

_____. *A Little Madness.* 1986. New York: Ballantine, 1987.

_____. *The Tanglewood Murder.* New York: Ballantine, 1981.

_____. *No Lady in the House.* New York: Ballantine, 1984.

Kenney, Susan. *Garden of Malice.* 1983. New York: Ballantine, 1984.

_____. *Graves in Academe.* 1985. New York: Penguin, 1986.

McConnell, Vicki P. *The Burnton Widows.* Tallahassee: Naiad, 1984.

_____. *Mrs. Porter's Letter.* 1982. Tallahassee: Naiad, 1986.

Miner, Valerie. *Murder in the English Department.* Freedom, CA: Crossing, 1982.

Moore, Maureen. *Fieldwork.* Seattle: Seal, 1987.

Muller, Marcia. *Ask the Cards a Question.* New York: St. Martin's, 1982.

_____. *The Cavalier in White.* New York: St. Martin's, 1986.

_____. *Edwin of the Iron Shoes.* New York: David McKay, 1977.

_____. *Games to Keep the Dark Away.* New York: St. Martin's, 1984.

_____. *Leave a Message for Willie.* New York: St. Martin's, 1984.

_____. *The Legend of the Slain Soldiers.* 1985. New York: Signet, 1987.

_____. *There's Nothing to Be Afraid Of.* New York: St. Martin's, 1985.

_____. *The Tree of Death.* 1983. New York: Signet, 1987.

Muller, Marcia, and Bill Pronzini. *Beyond the Grave.* New York: Walker, 1986.

O'Donnell, Lillian. *Ladykiller.* New York: Putnam's, 1984.

_____. *No Business Being a Cop.* New York: Putnam's, 1979.

Paretsky, Sara. *Bitter Medicine.* New York: Morrow, 1987.

_____. *Deadlock.* 1984. New York: Ballantine, 1985.

_____. *Indemnity Only.* 1982. New York: Ballantine, 1983.

_____. *Killing Orders.* 1985. New York: Ballantine, 1986.

Paul, Barbara. *The Renewable Virgin.* 1985. New York: Bantam, 1986.

Rich, Virginia. *The Baked Bean Supper Murders.* 1983. New York: Ballantine, 1984.

_____. *The Nantucket Diet Murders.* New York: Delacorte, 1985.

Sayers, Dorothy. *Gaudy Night.* 1935. New York: Avon, 1968.

_____. *Have His Carcase.* 1932. New York: Avon, 1968.

_____. *Strong Poison.* 1930. New York: Avon, 1967.

Silver, Victoria. *Death of a Harvard Freshman.* New York: Bantam, 1984.

_____. *Death of a Radcliffe Roommate.* New York: Bantam, 1986.

Smith, Joan. *A Masculine Ending.* New York: Scribner's, 1988.

Taylor, Elizabeth Atwood. *Murder at Vassar.* 1987. New York: Ballantine, 1988.

Wilson, Barbara. *Murder in the Collective*. Seattle: Seal, 1984.
_____. *Sisters of the Road*. Seattle: Seal, 1986.

SECONDARY WORKS CITED

Abel, Elizabeth, Marianne Hirsch, and Elizabeth Langland, eds. *The Voyage In: Fictions of Female Development*. Hanover, NH: Univ. Press of New England, 1983.

Aisenberg, Nadya, and Mona Harrington. *Women of Academe: Outsiders in the Sacred Grove*. Amherst: Univ. of Massachusetts Press, 1988.

Arden, Leon. "A Knock at the Backdoor of Art: The Entrance of Raymond Chandler." *Art in Crime Writing*. Edited by Bernard Benstock. New York: St. Martin's, 1983. 73–96.

Bakerman, Jane. "Cordelia Gray: Apprentice and Archetype." *Clues* 5 (1984): 101–14.

Bakhtin, Mikhail. *The Dialogic Imagination: Four Essays*. Ed. Michael Holquist. Trans. Caryl Emerson and Michael Holquist. Austin: Univ. of Texas Press, 1981.

Bargainnier, Earl, ed. *Ten Women of Mystery*. Bowling Green: Bowling Green State Univ. Popular Press, 1981.

Baym, Nina. *Woman's Fiction: A Guide to Novels by and about Women in America, 1820–1870*. Ithaca: Cornell Univ. Press, 1978.

Brontë, Charlotte. *Villette*. 1853. New York: Bantam, 1986.

Campbell, SueEllen. "The Detective Heroine and the Death of Her Hero: Dorothy Sayers to P. D. James." *Modern Fiction Studies* 29 (1983): 497–510.

Chodorow, Nancy. *The Reproduction of Mothering: Psychoanalysis and the Sociology of Gender*. Berkeley: Univ of California Press, 1978.

Cirile, Marie. *Detective Marie Cirile: Memoirs of a Police Officer*. New York: Doubleday, 1975.

Daly, Mary. *Gyn/Ecology*. Boston: Beacon, 1978.

Delmar, Rosalind. "What is Feminism?" Mitchell and Oakley, 8–33.

Dinnerstein, Dorothy. *The Mermaid and the Minotaur: Sexual Arrangements and Human Malaise*. 1976. New York: Harper & Row, 1977.

Donovan, Josephine. "Toward a Women's Poetics." *Feminist Issues in Literary Scholarship*. Edited by Shari Benstock. Bloomington: Indiana Univ. Press, 1987. 98–109.

Dworkin, Andrea. *Right-Wing Women: The Politics of Domesticated Females*. New York: Putnam, 1983.

Eisenstein, Hester. *Contemporary Feminist Thought*. Boston: G. K. Hall, 1983.

Faderman, Lillian. *Surpassing the Love of Men: Romantic Friendship and Love between Women from the Renaissance to the Present*. New York: Morrow, 1981.

Ferguson, Ann, Jacqueline N. Zita, and Kathryn Pyne Addelson. "On 'Compulsory Heterosexuality and Lesbian Existence': Defining the

Issues." *Feminist Theory: A Critique of Ideology.* Edited by Nannerl O. Keohane, Michelle Z. Rosaldo, and Barbara C. Gelpi. Chicago: Univ. of Chicago Press, 1982. 147–88.

Fetterly, Judith. *The Resisting Reader: A Feminist Approach to American Fiction.* Bloomington: Indiana Univ. Press, 1978.

Flynn, Elizabeth A., and Patrocinio P. Schweickart, eds. *Gender and Reading.* Baltimore: Johns Hopkins Univ. Press, 1986.

Gardiner, Judith Kegan. "On Female Identity and Writing by Women." *Writing and Sexual Difference.* Edited by Elizabeth Abel. Chicago: Univ. of Chicago Press, 1982. 177–91.

Gilbert, Sandra, and Susan Gubar. *The Madwoman in the Attic: The Woman Writer and the Nineteenth-Century Literary Imagination.* New Haven: Yale Univ. Press, 1979.

Gilligan, Carol. *In a Different Voice.* Cambridge: Harvard Univ. Press, 1982.

Gorham, Deborah. *The Victorian Girl and the Feminine Ideal.* Bloomington: Indiana Univ. Press, 1982.

Grella, George. "The Hard-boiled Detective Novel." *Detective Fiction.* Edited by Robin W. Winks. Englewood Cliffs, NJ: Prentice-Hall, 1980.

Heilbrun, Carolyn G. *Reinventing Womanhood.* New York: Norton, 1979.

Hughes, Winifred. *The Maniac in the Cellar.* Princeton; Princeton Univ. Press. 1980.

Janeway, Elizabeth. *Powers of the Weak.* New York: Knopf, 1980.

Jones, Ann Rosalind. "Writing the Body: Toward an Understanding of l'Écriture feminine." *The New Feminist Criticism.* Edited by Elaine Showalter. New York: Pantheon, 1985. 361–77.

Joyner, Nancy C. "P. D. James." Bargainnier, 109–123. (See above.)

Kennard, Jean E. "Ourself Behind Ourself: A Theory for Lesbian Readers." Flynn and Scweickart, 63–80. (See above.)

Klein, Kathleen Gregory. "Dorothy Sayers." Bargainnier, 8–39. (See above.)

Knepper, Marty S. "Agatha Christie—Feminist." *The Armchair Detective.* 16 (1983): 398–406.

Knox, Ronald. "A Detective Story Decalogue." *Detective Fiction.* Edited by Robin W. Winks. Englewood Cliffs, NJ: Prentice-Hall, 1980. 200–202.

Lawrence, Barbara. "Female Detectives: The Feminist-Anti-Feminist Debate." *Clues* 3 (1982): 38–48.

MacKinnon, Catharine A. *Sexual Harassment of Working Women: A Case of Sex Discrimination.* New Haven: Yale Univ. Press, 1979.

Marcus, Steven. "Dashiell Hammett." *The Poetics of Murder.* Edited by Glenn W. Most and William W. Stowe. New York: Harcourt, 1983. 197–209.

Mitchell, Juliet, and Ann Oakley, eds. *What Is Feminism? A Re-Examination.* New York: Pantheon, 1986.

Modleski, Tania. *Loving with a Vengeance.* New York: Methuen, 1982.

Naremore, James. "Dashiell Hammett and the Poetics of Hard-Boiled Detection." *Art in Crime Writing*. Edited by Bernard Benstock. New York: St. Martin's, 1983. 49–72.

O'Brien, Geoffrey. *Hard-Boiled America*. New York: Van Nostrand Reinhold, 1981.

Pederson-Krag, Geraldine. "Detective Stories and the Primal Scene." *The Poetics of Murder*. Edited by Glenn W. Most and William W. Stowe. New York: Harcourt, 1983. 13–20.

Pennell, Jane. "The Female Detective: Pre- and Post-Women's Lib." *Clues* 6 (1985): 85–98.

Pratt, Annis. *Archetypal Patterns in Women's Fiction*. Bloomington: Indiana Univ. Press, 1981.

Rich, Adrienne. "Compulsory Heterosexuality and Lesbian Existence." *The Signs Reader: Women, Gender, and Scholarship*. Edited by Elizabeth Abel and Emily K. Abel. Chicago: Univ. of Chicago Press, 1983. 139–68.

_____. "Husband-Right and Father-Right." *On Lies, Secrets, and Silence*, 215–22. New York: Norton, 1979.

_____. "The Meaning of Our Love for Women Is What We Have Constantly to Expand." *On Lies*, 223–30. (See above.)

_____. *Of Woman Born: Motherhood as Experience and Institution*. 1976. New York: Bantam, 1977.

Roberts, Jeanne Addison. "Feminist Murder: Amanda Cross Reinvents Womanhood." *Clues* 6 (1985): 2–13.

Ruddick, Sara. "Maternal Thinking." *Feminist Studies* 6 (1980): 342–67.

Russ, Joanna. *How to Suppress Women's Writing*. Austin: Univ. of Texas Press, 1983.

Shapiro, Laura. "Sara Paretsky." *Ms.* (January 1988): 66ff.

Showalter, Elaine. "Critical Cross-dressing: Male Feminists and the Woman of the Year." *Raritan* 2 (1983): 130–49.

_____. *A Literature of Their Own*. Princeton: Princeton Univ. Press, 1977.

Spender, Dale. *Mothers of the Novel*. New York: Pandora, 1986.

Stimpson, Catherine. "Zero Degree Deviancy: The Lesbian Novel in English." *Writing and Sexual Difference*. Edited by Elizabeth Abel. Chicago: Univ. of Chicago Press, 1982. 243–59.

Symons, Julian. *Bloody Murder*. 1972. New York: Penguin, 1985.

Zimmerman, Bonnie K. "Exiting from Patriarchy: The Lesbian Novel of Development." Abel, Hirsch, and Langland, 244–57.

_____. "What Has Never Been: An Overview of Lesbian Feminist Criticism." *The New Feminist Criticism*. Edited by Elaine Showalter. New York: Pantheon, 1985. 200–24.

Index